PLEASE EXPLAIN

Houghton Mifflin books on
science and mathematics by
ISAAC ASIMOV

Words of Science
More Words of Science
Realm of Numbers
Realm of Measure
Breakthroughs in Science
Realm of Algebra
The Human Body
The Human Brain
Quick and Easy Math
An Easy Introduction to the Slide Rule
Great Ideas of Science
Please Explain

PLEASE
EXPLAIN
BY ISAAC
ASIMOV

Decorations by Michael McCurdy

HOUGHTON MIFFLIN COMPANY 1973

To Richard F. Dempewolff

Library of Congress Cataloging in Publication Data

Asimov, Isaac, 1920-
  Please explain.

  SUMMARY: Answers to questions in various scientific
disciplines, e.g., "What are pulsars?", "Is the
universe running down?", "What is the difference between
a brain and a computer?", and "Why did the dinosaurs die
off?".
    1. Science--Juvenile literature.   [1. Science.
2. Questions and answers—Science]   I. McCurdy,
Michael, illus.   II. Title.
Q163.A85   500   73-7908
ISBN 0-395-17517-8

FIRST PRINTING   V

Table of Contents

PLEASE
EXPLAIN

Introduction

Back in 1965, that estimable magazine *Science Digest* began a new department titled "Please Explain." Its purpose was to select questions from among those sent in by readers and answer them in 500 words or so.

The magazine asked if I would tackle an occasional question for a reasonable sum of money. "Well," I said dubiously, "an *occasional* question."

I might have guessed. The occasional question became a monthly one and the department "Please Explain" became "Isaac Asimov Explains." (To avoid the possible pitfall of my well-known modesty, the change was made without consulting me.) Before I knew it, I had been at it for over eight years and had accumulated a hundred questions and answers.

And who could then resist collecting the essays and making a book out of it? Not I! And not Houghton Mifflin, either!

Since the answers I am asked to give depend on the questions the readers ask, the essays are not uniformly spread over the entire field of science. The readers are profoundly interested in theoretical physics for some reason, and questions involving speed of light and subatomic particles are particularly numerous.

Consequently, there is some duplication among the answers, and some glaring omissions.

Both have their advantages. The duplications come about, in part, because I have tried to make each answer complete in itself as far as possible. You can therefore turn to any question that strikes your fancy and read the book in any order you please.

As for the omissions — well, what's wrong with having them rouse a healthy curiosity? If the curiosity is healthy enough, send in a question of your own to *Science Digest*. If I get a chance (and if I know enough) I will answer it, and eight years hence there could be enough material to put out a book entitled "Isaac Asimov Explains Some More."

1

1

What is the scientific method?

Obviously the scientific method is the method used by scientists in making scientific discoveries. This doesn't seem to be a helpful definition, however. Can we go into detail?

Well, one can describe an ideal version of the method:

1. Recognize that a problem exists — as, for instance, the question of why objects move as they do, speeding up under some conditions, slowing down under others.

2. Sort out and discard the nonessential aspects of the problem. For instance, the smell of an object plays no part in its motion.

3. Gather all the data you can find that bear on the problem. In ancient and medieval times, this merely meant the keen observation of nature as it existed. In early modern times, the notion arose that nature could be helped out. One could deliberately design a situation in which objects would be made to behave in such a way as to yield data bearing on the problem. One could deliberately roll balls down inclined planes, varying the size of the balls, the nature of their surface, the inclination of the plane, and so on. Such deliberately designed situations are experiments, and the role of experiment is so central to modern science that it is sometimes spoken of as "experimental science" to distinguish it from the science of the ancient Greeks.

4. With all the data gathered, work up some tentative generalization that describes them all as simply as possible — some short statement or some mathematical relationship. This is an hypothesis.

5. With the hypothesis in hand, you can predict the results of experiments you had not thought to try earlier. Try them and see whether the hypothesis holds up.

2

6. If the experiments work as expected, the hypothesis is strengthened thereby and may attain the status of a theory or even a "natural law."

No theory or natural law is final, of course. The process repeats and repeats. New data, new observations, new experiments are continually being made. Old natural laws are constantly being superseded by more general ones that will explain everything the old one explained, and more.

All this, as I say, is an *ideal* version of the scientific method. In actual practice, scientists need not go through it like a set of calisthenic exercises, and usually don't.

More than anything else, such factors as intuition, insight, and just plain luck play a part. The history of science is full of cases of scientists who make a sudden inspired guess based on very inadequate data and on little or no experimentation and come upon a helpful truth that might have taken years to attain by straightforward slogging through the ideal scientific method.

F. A. Kekulé caught the structure of benzene while dozing on a bus. Otto Loewi awoke in the middle of the night with the answer to the problem of synapse conduction. Donald Glaser was glancing idly at his glass of beer and got the idea for the bubble chamber.

Does that mean that it's all luck, after all, and no brains? No, no, a thousand times no. This kind of "luck" happens only to the *best* brains; only to those whose "intuition" is the reward of great experience, deep understanding, and hard thought.

2

Who, in your opinion, was the greatest scientist who ever lived?

If the question were "Who was the second greatest scientist?" it would be impossible to answer. There are at least a dozen men who, in my opinion, could make a claim to second place. Included, for instance, would be Albert Einstein, Ernest Rutherford, Niels Bohr, Louis Pasteur, Charles Darwin, Galileo Galilei, J. Clerk Maxwell, Archimedes, and others.

In fact, it is very likely that there isn't a second greatest scientist at all. The claims of so many are so good and the difficulty of distinguishing levels of merit are so great that we might end up by declaring, say, a ten- or twelve-place tie.

But since the question is "Who is the *greatest?*" there is no problem. I feel that most historians of science would declare at once that Isaac Newton was the greatest scientific mind the world has even seen. He had his faults, heaven knows: he was a poor lecturer, something of a moral coward and self-pitying sniveler, and was at times subject to serious breakdowns. But as a *scientist,* he has no equal.

He founded higher mathematics by working out the calculus. He founded modern optics by his experiments on breaking up white light into the colors of the spectrum. He founded modern physics by stating the laws of motion and deducing their consequences. He founded modern astronomy by working out the law of universal gravitation.

Any one of these four feats, taken by itself, would have been sufficient to show him to be a scientist of major importance. All four, taken together, put him in first place without any question.

Nor are his discoveries all there is to say about Newton. His manner of presenting them was even more important.

The ancient Greeks had put together a formidable collection of scientific and philosophic thought. For two thousand years names such

4

as Plato, Aristotle, Euclid, Archimedes, and Ptolemy had towered like giants over the generations that followed. The great thinkers among the Arabs and Europeans harked back to the Greeks and scarcely ever dared advance any notion of their own without buttressing it by a reference to the ancients. Aristotle in particular was the "master of those who know."

In the sixteenth and seventeenth centuries, a number of experimenters such as Galileo and Robert Boyle demonstrated that the ancient Greeks did *not* have all the right answers. Galileo shattered Aristotle's notions about physics, for instance, doing the work that Newton later summarized in his three laws of motion. Nevertheless, Europe's intellectuals still dared not break away from the long-idolized Greeks.

Then came 1687, when Newton published his Latin-language *Principia Mathematica* (the greatest single scientific book ever written, in the opinion of most scientists). In it, he presented his laws of motion, his theory of gravitation, and many other things, making use of mathematics in the strict Grecian style and organizing everything in the most faultlessly elegant manner. Those who read the book had to admit that here, at last, was a mind that was the equal or superior of any of the ancients, and that the world picture he presented was beautiful, complete, and infinitely superior in rationality and inevitability than anything in the Greek books.

With that one man and book, the hold of the ancients was smashed and modern man's intellectual inferiority complex was forever broken.

After Newton's death, Alexander Pope said it all in two lines:

Nature and Nature's laws lay hid in night:
God said, Let Newton be! and all was light.

3

Why do two or more scientists who are unaware of one another's work often hit upon the same theory at the same time?

The simplest way of answering this is to say that scientists do not work in a vacuum. They are all embedded, so to speak, in the structure and developing progress of science, and are all faced with the same problems at the same time.

Thus, in the first half of the nineteenth century, the matter of evolution of species was very much "in the air." Some biologists were hotly against the very notion, while others speculated avidly on the consequences of such evolution and on finding evidence for it. The point is, though, that in one way or another, almost every biologist was thinking about the matter. The key problem was this:

If evolution takes place, what causes it to take place?

In Great Britain, Charles Darwin was thinking about this. In the East Indies, another Englishman, Alfred Wallace, was thinking about the same problem. Both had been world travelers; both had made similar observations; and both at a crucial point in their thinking happened to read a book by Thomas Malthus which described the effects of population pressure on human beings. Both Darwin and Wallace began to think about population pressure on all species. Which individuals would survive, which would not? Both came up with the theory of evolution by natural selection.

This is not at all surprising, really. Two men working on the same problem in the same way, faced with the same facts to observe, and with the same books written by others, might very likely come up with the same answers. What surprises me much more is that Darwin, Wallace, and Malthus all had the middle initial R.

In the latter part of the nineteenth century, many biologists were

6

trying to work out the mechanics of genetics. Three men, all working on the same problem at the same time and in the same way, but in three different countries, came to the same conclusion. But then each one, looking back through the literature, discovered that someone else, Gregor Mendel, had worked out the laws of heredity thirty-four years earlier and had been ignored.

One of the great challenges of the 1880s was the cheap production of aluminum. The nature and uses of the metal were known, but it was difficult to prepare it from its ores. Literally millions of dollars depended on the development of an easy technique. It's hard to say how many different chemists all worked on the same problem, with the same experiences of other chemists to draw upon. Two of them, Charles Hall in the United States and Paul Héroult in France, came up with the same answer in the same year, 1886. That's only natural, but how about this: both had names beginning with H, both were born in 1863, and both died in 1914.

Right now, many people are trying to work out theories to explain the behavior of subatomic particles. Murray Gell-Man and Yuval Ne'emen, one in America and one in Israel, came up with similar theories simultaneously. The principle of maser was worked out in the United States and the Soviet Union simultaneously. And I'm pretty sure the key process for the future use of practical fusion power will be worked out independently by two or more people simultaneously.

Of course, sometimes lightning strikes only once. Gregor Mendel had no competition; nor had Newton nor Einstein. Their greatest ideas occurred only to them, and the rest of the world followed.

4

What is Gödel's proof? Does it show truth is unobtainable?

Ever since the time of Euclid, 2200 years ago, mathematicians have tried to begin with certain statements called "axioms" and then deduce from them all sorts of useful conclusions.

In some ways it is almost like a game, with two rules. First, the axioms must be as few as possible. If you can deduce one axiom from the others, that deduced axiom must be dropped. Second, the axioms must be self-consistent. It must never be possible to deduce two conclusions from the axioms with one the negative of the other.

Any high school geometry book begins with a set of axioms: that through any two points only one straight line can be drawn; that the whole is equal to the sum of the parts, and so on. For a long time, it was assumed that Euclid's axioms were the only ones that could build up a self-consistent geometry so that they were "true."

In the nineteenth century, however, it was shown that Euclid's axioms could be changed in certain ways and that different, "non-Euclidean geometries" could be built up as a result. Each geometry was different from the others, but each was self-consistent. After that it made no sense to ask which was "true." One asked instead which was useful.

In fact, there are many sets of axioms out of which a self-consistent system of mathematics could be built, each one different, each one self-consistent.

In any such system of mathematics you must not be able to deduce from its axioms that something is *both* so *and* not so, for then the mathematics would not be self-consistent and would have to be scrapped. But what if you make a statement and find that you can't prove it to be *either* so *or* not so?

Suppose that I say, "The statement I am now making is false!"

Is it false? If it is false, then it is false that I am saying something false and I must be saying something true. But if I am saying something true then it is true that I am saying something false, and I am indeed saying something false. I can go back and forth forever. It is impossible to show that what I have said is *either* so *or* not so.

Suppose you adjust the axioms of logic to eliminate the possibility of my making statements like that. Can you find some other way of making such neither-so-nor-not-so statements?

In 1931, an Austrian mathematician, Kurt Gödel, presented a valid proof that showed that for any set of axioms you can always make statements that cannot be shown to be so from those axioms and yet cannot be shown to be not so either. In that sense, it is impossible to work out, ever, a set of axioms from which you can deduce a *complete* mathematical system.

Does that mean that we can never find "truth"? Not at all!

First: Just because a mathematical system isn't complete doesn't mean that what it does contain is "false." Such a system can still be extremely useful, provided we do not try to use it beyond its limits.

Second: Gödel's proof applies only to deductive systems of the types used in mathematics. But deduction is not the only way to discover "truth." No axioms can allow us to deduce the dimensions of the solar system. Those dimensions were obtained by observations and measurements — another route to "truth."

5

What is the difference between ordinary numbers and binary numbers and what are the advantages of each?

The ordinary numbers we use are "10-based." That is, they are written as powers of ten. What we write as 7291 is really 7×10^3 plus 2×10^2 plus 9×10^1 plus 1×10^0. Remember that $10^3 = 10 \times 10 \times 10 = 1000$; that $10^2 = 10 \times 10 = 100$; that $10^1 = 10$; and $10^0 = 1$. Therefore, 7291 is 7×1000 plus 2×100 plus 9×10 plus 1. We say this when we read the number aloud. It is "seven thousand two hundred ninety (nine tens) one."

We have grown so accustomed to the use of powers of ten that we just write the digits by which they are multiplied, 7291 in this case, and ignore the rest.

But there is no magic about powers of ten. The power of any other number higher than one would do. Suppose, for instance, we wanted to write the number 7291 in terms of powers of eight. Remember that $8^0 = 1$; $8^1 = 8$; $8^2 = 8 \times 8 = 64$; $8^3 = 8 \times 8 \times 8 = 512$; and $8^4 = 8 \times 8 \times 8 \times 8 = 4096$. The number 7291 can then be written as 1×8^4 plus 6×8^3 plus 1×8^2 plus 7×8^1 plus 3×8^0. (Work it out and see for yourself.) If we write only the digits, we have 16173. We can say, then, that 16173 (8-based) = 7291 (10-based).

The advantage of the 8-based system is that you only need to memorize seven digits besides 0. If you try to use the digit 8, you might have 8×8^3 which is equal to 1×8^4, so you can always use a 1 instead of an 8. Thus 8 (10-based) = 10 (8-based); 89 (10-based) = 131 (8-based); and so on. On the other hand there are more total digits to the number in the 8-based system than in the 10-based system. The smaller the base, the fewer different digits but the more total digits.

If you used a 20-based system, the number 7291 becomes 18×20^2

plus 4×20^1 plus 11×20^0. If you wrote 18 as # and 11 as % you could say that #4% (20-based) = 7291 (10-based). You would have to have 19 different digits in a 20-based system but you would have fewer total digits per number.

Ten is a convenient base. It gives us not too many different digits to remember and not too many separate digits in a given number.

What about a number based on powers of two — a 2-based number? It is this which is a "binary number," from a Latin word meaning "two at a time."

The number, 7291 equals 1×2^{12} plus 1×2^{11} plus 1×2^{10} plus 0×2^9 plus 0×2^8 plus 0×2^7 plus 1×2^6 plus 1×2^5 plus 1×2^4 plus 1×2^3 plus 0×2^2 plus 1×2^1 plus 1×2^0. (Work it out and see, remembering that 2^9, for instance, is nine twos multiplied together: $2 \times 2 \times 2 \times 2 \times 2 \times 2 \times 2 \times 2 \times 2 = 512$.) If we write only the digits we have 1110001111011 (2-based) = 7291 (10-based).

Binary numbers contain only 1's and 0's, so that addition and multiplication are fantastically simple. However, there are so many digits altogether in even small numbers like 7291 that it is fantastically easy for the human mind to become confused.

A computer, however, can use a two-way switch. In one direction, current on, it can symbolize a 1; in the other direction, current off, a 0. By manipulating the circuits so that the switches turn on and off in accordance with binary rules of addition and multiplication, the computer can perform arithmetical computations very quickly. It can do it much more quickly than if it had to work with gears marked from 0 to 9 as in ordinary desk calculators based on the decimal or 10-based system.

11

6

What are imaginary numbers?

There are two kinds of numbers that most of us are familiar with: positive numbers ($+5$, $+17.5$) and negative numbers (-5, -17.5). Negative numbers were introduced in the Middle Ages to take care of problems like $3 - 5$. To the ancients it seemed impossible to subtract five apples from three apples. The medieval bankers, however, had a clear notion of debt. "Give me five apples. I only have money for three, but I will owe you for two," which is like saying $(+3) - (+5) = (-2)$.

Positive and negative numbers can be multiplied according to certain strict rules. A positive number multiplied by a positive number gives a positive product. A positive number multiplied by a negative number gives a negative product. And, most important, a negative number multiplied by a negative number gives a *positive* product.

Thus: $(+1) \times (+1) = (+1)$; $(+1) \times (-1) = (-1)$; and $(-1) \times (-1) = (+1)$.

Now suppose we ask ourselves: What number multiplied by itself gives us $+1$? Or, to phrase it more mathematically: What is the square root of $+1$?

There are two answers. One is $+1$, since $(+1) \times (+1) = (+1)$. The other answer is -1, since $(-1) \times (-1) = (+1)$. Mathematicians put this in their own shorthand by writing $\sqrt{+1} = \pm 1$.

Let's go on and ask: What is the square root of -1?

Here we are stuck. It isn't $+1$, because that multiplied by itself is $+1$. It isn't -1, either, because that multiplied by itself is $+1$, too. To be sure, $(+1) \times (-1) = (-1)$, but that is the multiplication of two *different* numbers and not a number multiplied by *itself*.

So we can invent a number and give it a special sign, say #1, defining it as follows: #1 is a number such that $(\#1) \times (\#1) = (-1)$.

When this notion was first introduced, mathematicians spoke of it as an "imaginary number" simply because it didn't exist in the system of numbers to which they were accustomed. Actually, it is no more imaginary than the ordinary "real numbers." The so-called imaginary numbers have carefully defined properties and can be manipulated as easily as the older numbers.

And yet because the new numbers were felt to be "imaginary" the symbol "i" was used. We can speak of positive imaginary numbers $(+i)$ and negative imaginary numbers $(-i)$, whereas $(+1)$ is a positive real number and (-1) a negative real number. Thus, we can say $\sqrt{-1} = \pm i$.

The system of real numbers can be exactly matched in the system of imaginary numbers. If we have $+5$, -17.32, $+3/10$, we can also have $+5i$, $-17.32i$, $+3i/10$.

You can even picture the imaginary system of numbers.

Suppose you represent the real number system on a straight line with 0 (zero) in the center. The positive numbers are on one side of the zero and the negative numbers are on the other.

You can then represent the imaginary system of numbers along another line, crossing the first at right angles at the zero point, with the positive imaginaries on one side of the zero and the negative imaginaries on the other. Numbers can be located anywhere in the plane by using both kinds together: $(+2) + (+3i)$ or $(+3) + (-2i)$. These are "complex numbers."

Mathematicians and physicists find it very useful to be able to associate all the points in a plane with a number system. They couldn't do without the so-called imaginary numbers.

7

What are prime numbers and why are mathematicians interested in them?

A prime number is any number that cannot be expressed as the product of two numbers other than itself and one. Thus $15 = 3 \times 5$, so 15 is not a prime number; and $12 = 6 \times 2 = 4 \times 3$, so 12 is not a prime number. On the other hand $13 = 13 \times 1$, and is not the product of any other pair of numbers, so 13 is a prime number.

There is no way of telling, just by looking at some numbers whether they are prime or not. You can tell at once that certain kinds of numbers are not prime. Any number, however long, which ends in a 2, 4, 5, 6, 8, or 0, or whose digits add up to a sum divisible by 3, is not a prime. However, if a number ends in 1, 3, 7, or 9, and if its digits do not add up to a sum divisible by 3, it may be prime — but it may not. There are no formulas that can tell us. You just have to try and see if you can make it the product of two smaller numbers.

One way of finding primes, hit or miss, is to begin by listing all the numbers beginning with 2 and going up as high as you can, say to 10,000. The first number is 2, which is prime. Leave that and then go up the list crossing out every second number. That removes all the numbers divisible by two, which are therefore not prime. The smallest number left after 2 is 3. That's the next prime and, leaving that in place, you cross out every third number thereafter to get rid of all the numbers divisible by 3. The next untouched number is 5 so you cross off every fifth number thereafter. The next is 7, every seventh; then 11, every eleventh; then 13 . . . and so on.

You might think that as you keep crossing out more and more numbers, you will finally reach a point where all the numbers greater than some particular number will be crossed out, so there will be no more prime numbers after some particular highest prime number. Actually,

14

this doesn't happen. No matter how high up we go into the millions or billions, there are always more prime numbers higher up that have escaped all the crossing-outs.

In fact, as long ago as 300 B.C., the Greek mathematician Euclid showed that no matter how high you go there must be prime numbers higher still. Suppose you take the first six prime numbers and multiply them together: $2 \times 3 \times 5 \times 7 \times 11 \times 13 = 30{,}030$. Now add 1 to get 30,031. That number cannot be divided evenly by either 2, 3, 5, 7, 11, or 13, since in each case you will get a result that will leave a remainder of 1. If 30,031 can't be divided by any number except itself, it is a prime number. If it can, then the numbers of which it is a product must be higher than 13. In fact, $30{,}031 = 59 \times 509$.

We can do this for the first hundred prime numbers or the first trillion, or the first any amount. If we calculate the product and add 1, the final figure is either a prime number itself or the product of prime numbers higher than those we've included in the list. No matter how far we go, there are prime numbers higher still, so that the number of prime numbers is infinite.

Every once in a while we come to pairs of consecutive odd numbers, both of which are prime: 5, 7; 11, 13; 17, 19; 29, 31; 41, 43. As high as mathematicians have looked, such prime pairs are found. Are there an infinite number of such prime pairs? *No one knows.* Mathematicians think so, but they have never been able to prove it. That's why they are interested in prime numbers. Prime numbers offer simple-sounding problems that are very hard to work out and mathematicians can't resist the challenge.

What use is it? *None;* but that just seems to increase the interest.

8

What would happen if an irresistible force met an immovable body?

This is a classic puzzler over which uncounted millions of arguments must have rolled their wordy way.

Before I give you my solution, however, let's make a few things clear. The game of exploring the universe by rational techniques, like any other game, must be played according to the rules. If two people are going to talk meaningfully together, they must agree on what the symbols they use (words or otherwise) are to be taken as meaning, and their comments must make sense in terms of that meaning.

All questions that do not make sense in terms of the definitions agreed upon are thrown out of court. There is no answer because the question must not be asked.

For instance, suppose I asked the question "How much does justice weigh?" (I might be thinking, perhaps, of the figure of a blinded Justice with scales in her hand.)

But weight is a property of mass and only material things have mass. (Indeed, matter may be most simply defined as "That which has mass.")

Justice is not a material thing, but an abstraction. By definition, mass is not one of its properties, so that to ask the weight of justice is to pose a meaningless question. It requires no answer.

Again, it is possible, by a series of very simple algebraic manipulations, to show that $1 = 2$. The only trouble is that in the course of this demonstration, we must divide by zero. In order to avoid such an inconvenient equality (to say nothing of a number of other demonstrations that would destroy the usefulness of mathematics) mathematicians have decided to make division by zero inadmissible in any

16

mathematical manipulation. The question, then, "What is the value of the fraction 2/0?" violates the rules of the game and is meaningless. It requires no answer.

Now we are ready for our irresistible force and our immovable body.

An "irresistible force" is, by definition (if words are to have any meaning at all), a force that cannot be resisted; a force that will move or destroy any body it encounters, *however great*, without being perceptibly weakened or deflected. In any universe that contains an irresistible force, there can be no such thing as an immovable body, since we have just defined an irresistible force as capable of moving *anything*.

An "immovable body" is, by definition (if words are to have any meaning at all), a body that cannot be moved; a body that will absorb any force it encounters, *however great*, without being perceptibly changed or damaged by the encounter. In any universe which contains an immovable body, there can be no such thing as an irresistible force, since we have just defined an immovable body as capable of resisting *any* force.

If we ask a question that implies the simultaneous existence of both an irresistible force and an immovable body, we are violating the definitions implied by the phrases themselves. This is not allowed by the rules of the game of reason. The question "What would happen if an irresistible force met an immovable body?" is therefore meaningless and requires no answer.

You might wonder if definitions can be so carefully made that no unanswerable questions can ever be asked. The answer is "No," as I explained in my answer to question 4.

9

How many particles are there in the universe?

Actually, there is no definite answer to that question, for no one really knows how large the universe is in the first place. However, let us make some assumptions.

One guess is that there are about 100,000,000,000 (or 10^{11} — a 1 followed by 11 zeros) galaxies in the universe. These galaxies are, on the average, each 100,000,000,000 (or 10^{11}) times as massive as our sun.

This means that the total quantity of matter in the universe is equal to $10^{11} \times 10^{11}$ or 10^{22} times the mass of the sun. In other words, there is enough matter in the universe to make 10,000,000,000,000,000,000,000 (ten sextillion) suns like ours.

The mass of our sun is equal to 2×10^{33} grams (where a gram is equal to about 1/28 of an ounce). This means that the total quantity of matter in the universe has a mass of $10^{22} \times 2 \times 10^{33}$ or 2×10^{55} grams. This can be written out as 20,000,000,000,000,000,000,000,000,-000,000,000,000,000,000,000,000,000. In words, that is 20 septendecillion grams.

Now let's work from the other end. The mass of the universe is concentrated almost entirely in the nucleons it contains. (The nucleons are the particles that are the chief components of the atomic nucleus.) The nucleons are tiny things and it takes 6×10^{23} of them to make up a mass of one gram.

Well, then, if 6×10^{23} nucleons make 1 gram and if there are 2×10^{55} grams in the universe, then the total number of nucleons in the universe is $6 \times 10^{23} \times 2 \times 10^{55}$ or 12×10^{78}. It would be more conventional to write this as 1.2×10^{79}.

Astronomers believe that 90 percent of the atoms in the universe is hydrogen, 9 percent is helium, and 1 percent consists of more complicated elements. A typical sample of 100 atoms, then, would consist of

18

90 hydrogen atoms, 9 helium atoms, and 1 (let us say) oxygen atom. The nuclei of the hydrogen atoms would contain 1 nucleon each — a proton. The nuclei of the helium atoms would contain 4 nucleons each — 2 protons and 2 neutrons. The nucleus of the oxygen atom would contain 16 nucleons — 8 protons and 8 neutrons.

The hundred atoms would therefore contain 142 nucleons altogether — 116 protons and 26 neutrons.

There is a difference between these two types of nucleons. The neutron has no electric charge and no companion particle need be considered. The proton has a positive electric charge, however, and since the universe, as a whole, is believed to be electrically neutral, there must be one electron (with a negative electric charge) in existence for every proton.

For every 142 nucleons, then, there are 116 electrons (to balance the 116 protons). To keep the proportion, the 1.2×10^{79} nucleons of the universe must be accompanied by 1×10^{79} electrons. Adding the nucleons and electrons, we have a total number of 2.2×10^{79} particles of matter in the universe. This can be written as 22,000,000,000,000,-000,000,000,000,000,000,000,000,000,000,000,000,000,000,-000,000,000,000,000,000 (or 22 quinvigintillion).

If the universe is half matter and half antimatter, then half those particles are antinucleons and antielectrons. That wouldn't affect the total number, however.

The only other particles present in vast quantities in the universe are photons, neutrinos, and, possibly, gravitons, but they are massless particles and I won't count them. Twenty-two quinvigintillion is quite enough, after all; it makes up a sizable universe.

10

Where did the substance of the universe come from?
What is beyond the edge of the universe?

The answer to the first question is simply that no one knows.

Science doesn't guarantee an answer to everything. It merely offers a system for working out an answer once enough information is obtained. As yet, we don't have the kind of information that would tell us where the substance of the universe came from.

We can speculate, however. I, myself, have imagined there might be something called "negative energy" just like ordinary "positive energy" except that equal quantities of "negative energy" and "positive energy" add together to form *nothing at all*. (Just as +1 and −1 add up to 0.)

In reverse, nothing at all might suddenly change into a glob of "positive energy" and an equal glob of "negative energy." If this is so, then the glob of "positive energy" may have developed into the universe we know and somewhere there is a corresponding "negative universe."

But why did nothing suddenly become two globs of opposite energies?

Why not? If $0 = (+1) + (−1)$, then something which is 0 might just as well become +1 and −1. Perhaps in an infinite sea of nothingness, globs of positive and negative energy in equal-sized pairs are constantly forming, and, after passing through evolutionary changes, combining once more and vanishing. We are in one of these globs in the period of time between nothing and nothing, and wondering about it.

All this, however, is just speculation. Scientists have never yet detected anything like "negative energy" or come across any reason for supposing it might exist, and until they do my idea has no value.

And what lies beyond the universe? Suppose I answer: nonuniverse. You may object that that doesn't mean anything and perhaps you're

right. On the other hand, there are many questions that do not have meaningful answers (as, for instance, "How high is up?") and these are "meaningless questions." Generally, scientists refuse even to consider meaningless questions.

But let's think about it anyway.

Suppose you were a highly intelligent ant who lived in the middle of the North American continent. In a lifetime of traveling, you had covered square yard upon square yard of land surface and had invented a spyglass that would let you see miles of additional land. Naturally, you would suppose the land went on forever.

But you might wonder if the land came to an end somewhere. If so, it raised a disturbing question: "If the land comes to an end, what would there be beyond the end?"

Mind you, your *only* experience is with land. You have never seen the ocean, have no concept of ocean, cannot visualize anything but land. Wouldn't you have to say, "If the land does indeed come to an end, then beyond it must lie nonland, whatever that is," and wouldn't you be right?

Well, if the universe is defined as the sum total of matter and energy and all the space it fills, then, if the universe does indeed have an end, beyond it is nonmatter and nonenergy immersed in nonspace; in short, nonuniverse, whatever that is.

And if the universe arose as a glob of positive energy formed, together with a glob of negative energy, out of nothing, then beyond the universe is nothing, which is just another way, perhaps, of saying nonuniverse.

11

Why does one talk of the "low temperature of space"? How can empty space have a temperature?

One shouldn't and it can't. Temperature is the average heat content per atom of a quantity of matter, and it is only matter that can have a temperature.

Suppose a body like the moon existed in space, light-years away from even the nearest star. If the surface of the moon were at 25° C. to begin with, it would lose heat by radiation continually, but it would also gain heat from the radiation of the distant stars. The radiation reaching it from the stars would be so small, however, as not to balance the loss through the moon's own radiation, and the temperature of its surface would begin to drop at once.

As the temperature of the moon's surface dropped, the rate of loss of heat by radiation would decrease steadily until finally, when the temperature was low enough, the radiation loss would be small enough to be balanced by absorption of radiation from the distant stars. The temperature of the moon's surface at that point would be small indeed, only slightly above absolute zero.

It is this low temperature of the moon's surface, far away from all stars, that is an example of what people think of when they speak of the "low temperature of space."

Actually the moon isn't far from all stars. It is quite close, less than 100 million miles, to one of them, the sun. If the moon were in its present position, but faced one side of the sun at all times, that side would absorb solar heat until its temperature at the center of the sunward face was far above the boiling point of water. Only at that high temperature would its own radiation loss balance the large solar influx.

The sun's heat would travel only exceedingly slowly through the insulating substance of the moon itself, and the surface facing away from the sun would get little heat, and radiate what little it got out into space. The night side would therefore be at the "low temperature of space."

But the moon rotates with respect to the sun so that every part of its surface gets only two weeks' worth of sunlight at a time. Under this limited period of radiation, the surface temperature of the moon reaches barely as high as the boiling point of water in particular places. During the long night, the temperature remains no less than 120 degrees above absolute zero (cold enough by our standards) at any time because before it can drop lower the sun rises again.

The earth is an entirely different case, because it has an atmosphere and an ocean. The ocean soaks up heat more efficiently than bare rock does and gives it up more slowly. It acts as a heat cushion, its temperature rising not so high under the sun nor falling so low in the sun's absence as that of land. Besides, the earth rotates so rapidly that most spots on its surface experience day or night only for a few hours at a time. In addition, earth's atmospheric winds carry heat from the day side to the night side and from the tropics to the poles.

It follows then that the earth experiences a range of temperatures far smaller than the moon does, even though both bodies are the same distance from the sun.

What would happen to a man exposed to the sub-Antarctic temperatures found on the night side of the moon? Not as much as you might think. Even though dressed in insulated clothing on earth, we lose body heat rather quickly to the atmosphere and its winds — which carry body heat away swiftly. The situation on the moon is quite different. There, in thermal space suit and boots, a man would experience little heat loss by conduction to the surface, or by convection to empty space with zero wind. He'd be in a thermos bottle sitting in a vacuum, radiating only small amounts of infrared. Cooling would be a slow process. His own body would, of course, be producing heat all the time, and he'd be more apt to feel too warm than too cold.

12

What is cosmic dust and where does it come from?

According to current astronomical views, the galaxies were originally vast conglomerations of gas and dust, which slowly rotated, broke into turbulent eddies, and condensed into stars. In some regions, where the stars formed thickly, virtually all the gas and dust found its way into one star or another. Little or none was left in the spaces between. This is true in globular clusters, in elliptical galaxies, and in the central core of spiral galaxies.

In the outskirts of the spiral galaxies, the process was much less efficient. Stars formed in fewer numbers and much gas and dust was left over. We are in the spiral arms of our own galaxy and we can see dust clouds making dark patches against the glow of the Milky Way. The center of our own galaxy is completely obscured by such clouds of dust.

The material out of which the universe is formed is mostly hydrogen and helium. Helium atoms have no tendency to stick together. Hydrogen atoms do, but only in pairs, forming hydrogen molecules (H_2). This means that most of the material between the stars consists of separate small helium atoms or separate small hydrogen atoms and molecules. These make up the interstellar gas that forms the bulk of the matter between the stars.

Interstellar dust (or cosmic dust), present in much smaller quantity, is made up of particles that are very tiny but much larger than single atoms or molecules, and must therefore contain atoms other than hydrogen or helium.

Next to hydrogen and helium, the most common type of atom in the universe is oxygen. It can combine with hydrogen to form hydroxyl groups (HO) and water molecules (H_2O). These will have a distinct tendency to cling to any other groups and molecules of the same sort

24

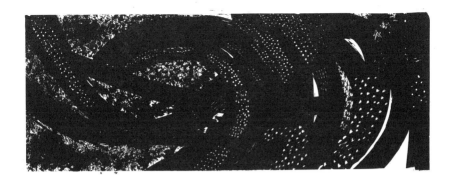

that they may encounter, so that gradually tiny particles made up of many millions of such molecules are built up. Hydroxyl groups and water molecules may make up a major part of the cosmic dust. It was only in 1965 that hydroxyl groups were actually detected in space and their distribution began to be studied. Since then, the existence of more complicated molecules, containing carbon atoms as well as hydrogen and oxygen, has also been reported.

Cosmic dust must also contain atom groupings made up of atoms even less common than hydrogen, oxygen, and carbon. Atoms of calcium, sodium, potassium, and iron have been detected in interstellar space, through the light they absorb.

Within our solar system, there is similar dust, contributed perhaps by comets. Outside the visible limits of our solar system, there may be a shell of large numbers of comets, some of which (through the gravitational effects of nearby stars, perhaps) drop down toward the sun. Comets are loose conglomerations of tiny solid fragments of metal and rock held together by a cement of ice plus frozen methane, ammonia, and other such materials. Each time a comet approaches the sun, some of its matter boils off and tiny solid particles are freed and scattered into space in the form of a long tail. Eventually, the comet breaks up altogether.

Countless comets have broken up in the history of the solar system and, as a result, the inner reaches of the system are littered with dust. Earth collects these dust particles ("micrometeoroids") by the billions each day. Space scientists are interested in them for a variety of reasons; for one thing, the larger micrometeoroids might present a hazard for future astronauts and moon colonists.

13

What are pulsars?

In the summer of 1967, rather by accident, Anthony Hewish and co-workers at Cambridge University detected radio emissions from the heavens that were like none ever detected before. They came in very regular pulses only 1 1/3 seconds apart. To be exact, they came 1.33730109 seconds apart. The source was called a "pulsating star" or "pulsar" for short.

Over the next couple of years a considerable number of such pulsars were discovered and you might wonder why they weren't discovered sooner. Each pulsar radiates considerable energy during a pulse, but the pulses are so brief that on the average the radio-wave intensity is very low, so it was missed. What was more, astronomers assumed that radio sources emitted energy at a steady level and didn't look for pulses.

A particularly rapid pulsar was discovered in the Crab Nebula and was found to be radiating in the visible-light range. It winked on and off just in time to the radio pulses. It had been observed many times before but had seemed just an ordinary star. No one had ever thought to test it with a detection device delicate enough to show it to be flashing on and off thirty times a second. With so rapid a pulse, the light seemed steady to the eye and to ordinary instruments.

But what *is* a pulsar? If an object emits energy at periodic intervals, then something physical must be happening to it at those intervals. It might be a body that is expanding and contracting, for instance, and emitting a burst of energy with each contraction. Or it might be rotating about its axis or revolving about another body and emitting a burst of energy with each rotation or revolution.

The difficulty was that the pulse is so very rapid, coming anywhere from every four seconds to every 1/30 of a second. The pulsar had to be a very hot body or it couldn't emit so much energy in the first place, and it had to be a very small body or it couldn't do anything at all so quickly.

The smallest hot body scientists had observed were white dwarf stars. These can be as massive as our sun — just as hot, too, or hotter — and yet are no larger than the earth. Was it possible that such white dwarf stars were producing pulses by expanding and contracting, or by rotating? Or could two white dwarf stars be revolving about each other? No matter how astronomers work the problem out theoretically, however, they couldn't make the white dwarfs move quickly enough.

But what about still smaller objects? Astronomers had theorized that it was possible for a star to contract so tightly under the pull of gravity as to force all the atomic nuclei in it to squash into contact. Electrons and protons would interact to form neutrons and the star would become a kind of neutron jelly. Such a "neutron star" would be as big as the sun and yet be only ten miles wide.

Neutron stars had never been observed, however, and they were so small that some astronomers feared that even if they existed they might be completely undetectable.

Yet such a small body could rotate rapidly enough to produce the pulses. There were conditions where electrons could escape only at certain points of its surface. As a neutron star rotated, the electrons would spray out like water from a rotating sprinkler, and once every rotation some would head out in our direction, producing radio waves and visible light.

Thomas Gold, of Cornell University, suggested that, if this were so, the neutron star would lose energy and the pulsations ought to slow up gradually. This was checked and found to be so. It seems very likely now that pulsars are the neutron stars astronomers feared they might never be able to detect.

14

They say that a cubic inch of a neutron star weighs billions of tons. How is that possible?

An atom is roughly 10^{-8} centimeters in diameter (or 1/250,000,000 of an inch across). In ordinary solids and liquids, the atoms are close together, virtually in contact. The density of ordinary solids and liquids depends, then, on the exact size of the atoms, the efficiency with which they are packed, and the weight of the individual atoms.

The least dense ordinary solid is frozen hydrogen, which is about 0.076 grams per cubic centimeter (or 0.014 ounces per cubic inch). The densest is the rare metal osmium, which is 22.48 grams per cubic centimeter (or 13 ounces per cubic inch).

If atoms were solid incompressible balls, osmium would be the densest material possible, and a cubic inch of matter could never even weigh a pound, let alone many tons.

But atoms aren't solid. As long ago as 1909, the New Zealand–born physicist Ernest Rutherford demonstrated that atoms were mostly empty space. The outskirts of atoms contain only very light electrons, and over 99.9 percent of the mass of the atom is concentrated in a tiny structure, the atomic nucleus, at the center.

The atomic nucleus has a diameter in the neighborhood of 10^{-13} centimeters (or roughly 1/100,000 that of the atom itself). If the atoms in a sphere of matter could be pushed together so hard that the electrons were shoved out of the way and the atomic nuclei were forced into contact, then the diameter of the sphere would decrease to only 1/100,000 of what it had been.

If the earth were compressed into a ball of atomic nuclei, all its matter would be forced into a sphere only 422 feet across. The sun, similarly compressed, would be 8.6 miles across. If all the known matter in the universe were converted into atomic-nuclei-in-contact, it would be a sphere only a couple of hundred million miles across and would fit comfortably within the asteroid belt of our solar system.

The heat and pressure at the center of stars break down atomic structure and allow the atomic nuclei to begin to pack together. Densities at the center of the sun are far higher than that of osmium, but the individual nuclei move about unhampered, and the material is still a gas. Some stars are made up almost entirely of such broken-down atoms. The companion of the star Sirius is a "white dwarf" no larger than the planet Uranus, yet just as massive as the sun.

Atomic nuclei are made up of protons and neutrons. The protons all have positive electric charges and repel each other, so that no more than a hundred or so can be brought together in any one place. The neutrons, however, are uncharged and, under the proper conditions, uncounted numbers can pack together to form a "neutron star." The pulsars are supposed to be such neutron stars.

If the sun were converted into a neutron star, all its mass would be squeezed into a ball $1/100,000$ its present diameter and $(1/100,000)^3$ or $1/1,000,000,000,000,000$ (one-quintillionth) its present volume. The density would therefore be $1,000,000,000,000,000$ (one quintillion) times what it is now.

The sun's present overall density is now 1.4 grams per cubic centimeter. As a neutron star, its density would be $1,400,000,000,000,000$ grams per cubic centimeter.

This means that one cubic inch of a neutron star could weigh as much as $25,000,000,000,000$ (25 thousand billion) tons.

15

What is a black hole?

To understand what a black hole is, let's begin with a star like our sun. The sun is 866,000 miles in diameter and has 330,000 times as much mass as the earth. Allowing for that mass and the distance from its surface to its center, anything on the surface of the sun would be subjected to a gravitational pull roughly 28 times earth's surface gravity.

An ordinary star is kept at its usual size by the balance between an enormously high central temperature which tends to expand the sun's substance and the enormous gravitational pull which tends to contract it and squeeze it together.

At some stage in its lifetime the internal temperature may fail, so that gravitation will take over. The star begins to collapse and in the process the atomic structure within it breaks down. In place of atoms are individual electrons, protons, and neutrons. It collapses to the point where the mutual repulsion of the electrons resists any further contraction.

The star is then a "white dwarf." A star like our sun, if it collapsed to a white dwarf, would squeeze all its mass into a sphere about 10,000 miles in diameter, and its surface gravity (subjected to the same mass but at a distance far closer to the center) would be 210,000 times the earth's.

Under certain conditions, the gravitational pull becomes too strong for even electron repulsion to resist. The star contracts again, forcing electrons and protons to combine to form neutrons, and shrinking to the point where all the neutrons are in contact. The neutron structure then resists further contraction and we have a "neutron star" which could contain all the mass of our sun in a sphere only 10 miles across. Its surface gravity would then be 210,000,000,000 times that of the earth.

Under certain conditions, gravitation can overcome even the resistance of neutron structure. In that case, there is nothing further that can resist collapse. The star can shrink to zero volume and the surface gravity can rise toward the infinite.

According to the theory of relativity, light emitted by a star loses some energy as it rises against the star's gravitational field. The more intense the field, the greater the energy loss. This has been checked by observation in the heavens and in the laboratory.

The light emitted by an ordinary star like the sun loses very little energy. The light emitted by a white dwarf loses more; and the light emitted by a neutron star still more. As the neutron star collapses further, there comes a point at which light rising from the surface loses *all* its energy and cannot escape.

Objects more compressed than neutron stars have so intense a gravitational field that anything that approaches them is trapped by them and can never get out again. It is as though the trapped object had fallen into an infinitely deep hole and never stopped falling. What's more, as I've just explained, even light cannot escape, so that the compressed object is black. It is, indeed, a "black hole."

Astronomers are now seeking some evidence of the actual existence of black holes here and there in the universe.

31

16

How hot can a star get?

It depends on the star, and on what part of a star you're considering.

Over 99 percent of the stars we can detect belong, like our sun, to a classification called "main sequence," and usually by the temperature of a star we mean the temperature of its surface. We'll begin there.

Any star has a tendency to collapse under its own gravitational pull, but as it collapses its interior grows hotter. As the interior grows hotter, the star has a tendency to expand. In the end, there is a balance and the star reaches some fixed size. The more massive a star, the greater the internal temperature must be to balance that collapsing tendency, and the higher the surface temperature in consequence.

Our sun, an average-size star, has a surface temperature of 6000° C. Stars with less mass have lower surface temperatures, some as low as 2500° C.

More massive stars have higher temperatures: 10,000° C., 20,000° C., and up. The most massive, and therefore the hottest and brightest stars known, have a steady surface temperature of at least 50,000° C., and possibly more. We might venture to say that the highest possible *steady* surface temperature of a main sequence star is 80,000° C.

Why not more? What about still more and more massive stars? Here we must call a halt. If an ordinary star gets so massive that its surface temperature is higher than 80,000° C., the extreme temperatures inside such a star will bring about an explosion. There might be momentarily much higher temperatures exposed, but when the explosion is over a smaller and cooler star will be left behind.

The surface is not the hottest part of a star, however. Heat is trans-

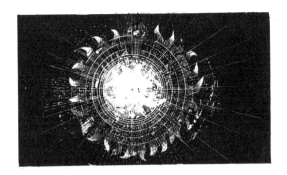

ferred outward from the surface to the thin atmosphere (or "corona") surrounding a star. The heat is not much in total quantity, but there are so few atoms in the corona, compared to the number in the star itself, that each atom gets a large supply. The heat energy per individual atom is what the temperature measures, and the sun's corona has, for that reason, a temperature of about 1,000,000° C.

The interior of a star is also much hotter than the surface. It must be, if it is to keep the outer layers of the star expanded against the enormous inward pull of gravity. It turns out that the core temperature of the sun is perhaps 15,000,000° C.

Naturally, a star more massive than the sun will have a higher core temperature as well as a higher surface temperature. Also, for a given mass, a star tends to grow hotter at the core as it ages. Some astronomers have tried to calculate how high the temperature can get at the core before the whole star blows apart. One estimate I have seen gives the maximum temperature as 6,000,000,000° C.

And what about objects that are not on the main sequence? In particular, what about objects newly discovered in the 1960s? There are pulsars, which are thought to be incredibly dense "neutron stars" with all the mass of an ordinary star packed into a sphere perhaps only ten miles across. Could their core temperatures reach beyond the six-billion-degree "maximum"? Or the quasars, which some people think may be a million or more ordinary stars all collapsed into one. What about their core temperatures?

So far, nobody knows.

17

In a star how far can fusion go?

When protons and neutrons combine to form an atomic nucleus, the combination is more stable and contains less mass than those same protons and neutrons separately. In forming the combination, the excess mass is converted to energy and radiated away.

One thousand tons of hydrogen, with nuclei made up of individual protons, are converted to 993 tons of helium, with nuclei made up of combinations of two protons and two neutrons. The missing 7 tons of mass is given off as its equivalent in energy.

Stars like our sun radiate energy formed in this way. The sun converts about 654,000,000 tons of hydrogen into a little under 650,000,000 tons of helium each second. It loses 4,600,000 tons of mass each second. Even at this huge rate, however, the sun contains enough hydrogen to keep it going for billions of years.

Yet someday the sun's hydrogen supply will approach exhaustion. Does that mean that fusion will stop and the sun will turn cold?

Not quite. Helium nuclei are not the ultimately economical packing of protons and neutrons. Helium nuclei can be fused to still more complicated nuclei, nuclei as complicated as those of iron, and more energy will be given off.

Not much more, though. The thousand tons of hydrogen that I have mentioned as fusing to 993 tons of helium can be further fused to 991.5 tons of iron. Seven tons of mass are converted to energy in passing from hydrogen to helium, only one and a half tons in passing from helium to iron.

And at iron we reach a dead end. In the iron nucleus, the protons and neutrons are packed with maximum stability. Any change in iron, in the direction of either simpler atoms or more complex ones, absorbs energy rather than emits it.

We can say, then, that by the time a star has reached helium it has given off about four-fifths of all the fusion energy that is available, and by moving on to iron, it gives off the remaining one-fifth, and that is all.

But what happens afterward?

In the process of passing to the stage of fusion beyond helium, the star's core gets much hotter. According to one theory it gets hot enough by the iron stage to take part in nuclear reactions that produce enormous quantities of neutrinos. Neutrinos are not absorbed by stellar material, so they streak away at the speed of light as soon as they form, carrying energy away with them. The core thus loses energy and cools down quite suddenly and the star collapses into a white dwarf star.

In the process of collapse, the outer layers, which still possess atoms less complicated than iron, fuse all at once, exploding into a "nova." The energies that result form some atoms more complicated than iron; atoms all the way to uranium and beyond.

The debris of such novas, containing the heavy atoms, mixes with interstellar gas, and stars formed out of such gas are "second-generation stars" containing small quantities of complex atoms they could never have formed through their own ordinary fusion. Our sun is a second-generation star; and that's why there is gold and uranium on the earth.

18

What happens to all the energy emitted by all the stars?

The stars emit energy in different ways:

1) As massless photons of electromagnetic radiation, from the most energetic gamma rays to the least energetic radio waves. (Even cold matter radiates photons; the colder the matter, the feebler the photons.) Visible light is part of this kind of radiation.

2) As other massless particles such as neutrinos and gravitons.

3) As massive charged particles of high energy, chiefly protons, but also including minor quantities of various atomic nuclei and still other kinds of particles. These are the cosmic rays.

All these emitted particles — photons, neutrinos, gravitons, protons, and so on — are stable as long as they are isolated in space. They can travel across billions of light-years of vacuum for billions of years of time without, as far as we can tell, undergoing any change.

All these radiated particles therefore exist until the time (however long that may be) when they strike some form of matter that will absorb them. In the case of photons, almost any matter will suffice. Energetic protons are stopped and absorbed with more difficulty, and neutrinos with a great deal more difficulty. About gravitons, very little is as yet known.

Suppose now that the universe consisted of nothing but stars in some unchanging configuration. Every particle emitted by one star would travel through space until it hit something else (another star) and was absorbed. Particles would just travel from star to star and, on the whole, every star would regain all the energy it had radiated away. It would seem then that the universe would continue unchanging forever.

That this is not so is the result of three things:

1) The universe is not made up of stars only, but contains a considerable amount of cold matter, from large planets to interstellar dust. When this cold matter stops some particle, it is absorbed and less energetic particles are given off in exchange. This means that on the whole the cold matter rises in temperature with time and the energy content of the stars decreases.

2) Some of the particles given off by stars, and by other forms of matter, too (such as neutrinos and gravitons), have so small a tendency to be absorbed by matter that through all the existence of the universe, only a tiny percentage of them has as yet been absorbed. This means that there is a constantly larger fraction of the total energy of the stars circling through space and this too means that the stars' energy content shrinks.

3) The universe is expanding. Each year there is more space between the galaxies so that even absorbable particles like protons and photons can travel longer distances, on the average, before striking matter and being absorbed. For this reason, too, each year sees less energy absorbed by stars than is emitted, and extra energy must go into filling the extra space, produced by expansion, with speeding, energetic, and, as yet, unabsorbed particles. In fact, this reason is sufficient by itself. As long as the universe continues to expand, it will continue to cool off on the whole.

Of course, if and when the universe begins to contract again, the situation will reverse itself, and it will begin to heat up again.

19

What is the solar wind?

As long ago as 1850 an English astronomer, Richard C. Carrington, who was studying sunspots, noticed a tiny flare-up on the face of the sun that was visible for about five minutes. Carrington thought he had happened to see the fall of a large meteor into the sun.

By the 1920s, the use of more sophisticated instruments for the study of the sun showed that such "solar flares" were common events, usually occurring in connection with sunspots. For instance, the American astronomer George E. Hale had invented the "spectroheliograph" in 1889 and this made it possible to observe the sun by the light of a particular wavelength. It was then possible to take a picture of the sun by the light of the glowing hydrogen in the sun's atmosphere, or the glowing calcium, for instance. It turned out that solar flares had nothing to do with meteorites, but were short-lived explosions of hot hydrogen.

Small flares are quite common and in places where there is a large complex of sunspots as many as a hundred a day can be detected, especially when the spots are growing. Very large flares, such as Carrington saw, are rare, and only a few occur each year.

Sometimes a flare takes place right in the center of the sun's disk, so that it explodes upward in the direction of the earth. Time and again after that happens, curious events take place on earth. Within days, there is a brightening of the Northern Lights, which are sometimes seen far down into the temperate regions. The magnetic compass acts up and becomes wildly variable, so that the effect is sometimes called a "magnetic storm."

Such events, prior to this century, didn't affect the general population much. In the twentieth century, however, it turned out that magnetic storms also affected radio reception and the behavior of electronic equipment generally. As mankind began to depend more and more on such equipment, magnetic storms became more important. During such a storm, for instance, radio and television transmission might break down and radar equipment refuse to work.

Astronomers studied the flares more carefully, and it became apparent that these explosions hurled hot hydrogen far upward and that some of it managed to be launched into space despite the sun's giant gravity. The hydrogen nuclei are simple protons, so that the sun is surrounded by a cloud of protons (and minor quantities of more complicated nuclei) spreading outward in all directions. In 1958, the American physicist Eugene N. Parker called this outward-streaming cloud of protons the "solar wind."

The protons streaming out in the direction of earth reach us and most are pushed around the planet by its magnetic field. Some enter the upper atmosphere, however, to cause the Northern Lights and to produce a variety of electrical phenomena. A particularly large flare, which shoots an intense cloud in our direction, will produce what we might call a temporary "solar gale" and the effects of the magnetic storm are produced.

It is the solar wind that is responsible for the tails of comets. The cloud of dust and gas about a comet moving near the sun is swept outward by the solar wind. Its effect has also been observed on man-made satellites. A large, light satellite, such as *Echo I*, was pushed perceptibly off its calculated orbit by the solar wind.

20

How long will the sun be able to sustain life on earth?

The sun will be able to sustain life (as we know it) on earth as long as it radiates energy in its present manner. We can set certain limits to how long this might be.

The radiation of the sun is produced by the fusion of hydrogen to helium. To produce all the radiation poured out by the sun, a vast amount of fusion must take place. Indeed, 630,000,000 tons of hydrogen must be fused to 625,400,000 tons of helium each second. (The 4,600,000 tons left over are converted into radiational energy and are lost to the sun forever. The tiny quantity of this energy that happens to hit the earth is sufficient to support all the life on our planet.)

It may seem that, with this quantity of hydrogen being consumed each second, the sun cannot last long — but that does not take into account the vast size of the sun. It has a mass of 2,200,000,000,000,000,-000,000,000,000 (over two billion billion billion) tons altogether. About 53 percent of this mass is hydrogen, which means that the sun now contains about 1,160,000,000,000,000,000,000,000,000 tons of hydrogen.

(If you are curious, the rest of the sun's mass is almost all helium. Less than 0.1 percent of its mass is made up of atoms more complicated than helium. Helium is more compact than hydrogen. Under identical conditions, a quantity of helium atoms would have four times as much mass as the same quantity of hydrogen atoms. A particular mass of helium, in other words, takes up less room than the same mass of hydrogen. In terms of volume — the room taken up — the sun is about 80 percent hydrogen.)

If we suppose that the sun was originally all hydrogen and that it has always been turning hydrogen into helium at the rate of 630 million

tons per second and will always continue doing so, then we can calculate that the sun has been radiating for roughly 40 billion years and will continue to radiate for another 60 billion.

Actually, things are not quite so simple. The sun is a "second-generation star," built up out of cosmic gas and dust left over by stars that had burnt and exploded billions of years before. The sun's raw material therefore contained much helium to begin with; almost as much as it now has. This means that the sun has only been radiating a short while, astronomically speaking, for its original hydrogen supply has declined only moderately. The sun may be no more than six billion years old.

Nor will the sun continue to radiate at exactly its present rate. The hydrogen and helium in the sun do not mix thoroughly. The helium is concentrated in the central core of the sun, and the fusion reaction takes place at the surface of this core.

As the sun continues radiating, the helium core gets more massive and the temperature at its center grows higher. Eventually, the temperature grows high enough there to force helium atoms into more complicated atoms. Till that point, the sun will radiate much as it does now, but after helium fusion begins it will begin to expand and gradually become a red giant. The heat on earth will become unbearable; the oceans will boil away, and the planet will no longer be an abode for life as we know it.

Astronomers estimate that the sun will enter this new phase about 8 billion years from now. Eight billion years is still a pretty long time, however, so there is no immediate cause for alarm.

21

If the temperature of the sun's surface is white hot,
why are sunspots black? They would have to be cold
to be black and how can anything on the sun be cold?

The question, as stated, would seem to be a real stopper. In fact, in the early 1800s, a great astronomer, William Herschel, decided that the sunspots must be cold since they were black. The only way he could explain this was to suggest that the sun wasn't hot all the way through. It had a white hot atmosphere, yes, but underneath that was a cold solid body and we could see that solid body through the rifts in the solar atmosphere. Those rifts we call sunspots. Herschel even thought the cool inner body of the sun might be inhabited by living things.

But this is wrong. We are quite sure now that the sun is hot all the way through. In fact, the surface we see is the coolest part of the sun and even that is surely too hot for living things.

Radiation and temperature are intimately related. In 1894, a German physicist, Wilhelm Wien, studied the kind of light radiated at different temperatures. He concluded that, under ideal conditions, every object, regardless of its chemical composition, radiated a particular range of light for each particular temperature.

As the temperature goes up, the wavelength of the peak radiation gets shorter and shorter in the same way for all bodies. At about 600° C. enough radiation slips down into the visible range to give the object a dull red appearance. Then, as the temperature goes higher still, the object becomes bright red, orange, white, and blue-white. (If the temperature were high enough, the radiation would be mostly in the ultraviolet and beyond.)

By carefully measuring the wavelength of the sun's radiation peak (it is in the yellow-light region), we can calculate the temperature of the sun's surface and it comes to about 6000° C.

42

The sunspots are *not* at this temperature. They are considerably cooler, and we can put the temperature at the center at only 4000° C. It seems that a sunspot represents a mighty expansion of gases, and such expansion, on the sun as in your refrigerator, causes a considerable temperature drop. It takes a huge heat pump to keep an enormous sunspot cool for days and weeks at a time against the heat flowing in from the surrounding hotter areas of the sun, and astronomers have not yet worked out a completely satisfactory mechanism for sunspot formation.

Even at 4000° C., the sunspots ought to be very bright. They should be considerably brighter than a carbon arc here on earth and a carbon arc is too bright to look at.

Well, the sunspot *is* brighter than a carbon arc and instruments check that out. The trouble is, though, that our eyes don't see light absolutely. We judge brightness by comparison with the environment. The hotter normal areas of the sun's surface are four to five times as bright as the cooler areas in the center of the sunspot, and, by comparing the latter with the former, the latter seems black to our eyes. That blackness is a kind of optical illusion.

That this is so can be sometimes demonstrated during an eclipse. The eclipsing moon, with its dark side toward us, is *really* black against the sun's bright globe. When the moon's edge encroaches over a large sunspot so that the spot's "darkness" can be seen right against the moon, it is possible to see that the spot is not really black.

22

Why are all the planets in approximately the same orbital plane?

The best astronomical guess is that they move in the same orbital plane because they were formed out of a single flat sheet of material.

Current theories suggest that the solar system was originally a vast mass of rotating dust and gas which may have been spherical to begin with. Under the influence of its own gravitational pull, it condensed and therefore had to spin more rapidly to conserve angular momentum.

As the cloud condensed more and more and rotated more and more rapidly, the centrifugal effect threw a portion of the matter outward from the equatorial plane. This outward-thrown matter, making up only a few percent of the whole, formed a large flat sheet around the main central portion of the cloud. Somehow (the details are by no means agreed upon) planets condensed out of the sheet, while the main portion of the cloud became the sun. The planets continued to circle through the region once occupied by that flat sheet and, for that reason, all revolve in about the same plane — the plane of the sun's equator.

For similar reasons, the planets, as they condensed, formed satellites which usually revolve in a single plane that coincides with that of the planet's equator.

Exceptions to this rule are thought to have resulted from violent events long after the general formation of the solar system. The planet Pluto revolves in a plane tilted at an angle of 17 degrees to earth's plane of revolution. (No other planet has an orbit so tilted.) Some astronomers speculate that Pluto may once have been a satellite of Neptune which was shaken loose by some undetermined cataclysm. Neptune's chief present satellite, Triton, does not revolve in the plane of

Neptune's equator, which is another sign of some cataclysm involving that planet.

Jupiter possesses seven small and distant satellites that do not revolve in the plane of its equator. Saturn's outermost satellite is in the same category. These satellites were probably not formed in their present position when the solar system came into being, but are asteroids captured long afterward by those giant planets.

Many of the asteroids that circle in orbits between those of Mars and Jupiter have orbital planes which are greatly tilted. Here, too, the signs point to catastrophe. It may well be that the asteroids were originally a single small planet circling in the general plane. Long after the formation of the solar system, an explosion, or series of explosions, may have fragmented that ill-fated world and sent the fragments flying into orbits that in many cases deviated widely from the general orbital plane.

Comets revolve in all possible planes. Some astronomers suspect, though, that there is a widespread cloud of comets on the far outskirts of the solar system, a light-year or so from the sun. These may have condensed from the outermost portions of the original spherical cloud before the general contraction began and before the equatorial sheet came into being.

When an occasional comet falls out of this spherical shell and into the inner regions of the solar system (as the result of the gravitational influence of distant stars, perhaps), it can therefore move around the sun in any plane.

23

How and why is Pluto different from all the other planets?

Pluto is noteworthy for being the most distant planet from the sun. (Its average distance is 3.6 billion miles.) But then, some planet has to be the most distant, and it just happens to be Pluto.

Yet that is not all. Pluto has certain unusual characteristics that set it apart from the eight other major planets and make it an object of considerable curiosity to astronomers. For instance:

(1) Pluto has the most elliptical orbit of any of the major planets. A perfect circle has an eccentricity of zero and the eccentricity of earth's orbit is only 0.017 so that it is close to circular. The eccentricity of Pluto's orbit, however, is 0.25. Sometimes it is as close as 2.7 billion miles to the sun; sometimes as far as 4.5 billion miles from it. In fact, when Pulto is at its closest to the sun, it is nearer than Neptune, and, for a while, is no longer the farthest planet. Right now, it is moving in closer than Neptune, and will stay closer for about forty years.

(2) Pluto has the most tilted orbit of any of the major planets. If all the planets were lined up in their orbits on the same side of the sun, they would all be just about one behind the other — all except Pluto. Pluto's orbit is tilted at 17 degrees to ours and it could be far above the general position of the other planets or far below. (That is why it could never hit Neptune when it crossed Neptune's orbit — it would cross it far above.)

(3) The eight planets other than Pluto fall into two groups. First, there are the four planets near the sun: Mercury, Venus, Earth, and Mars; all are small, dense and have comparatively little atmosphere. Then there are the four outer planets: Jupiter, Saturn, Uranus, and Neptune — giant planets, with low densities and enormous atmospheres. That leaves Pluto, which is out among the "gas giants," yet

is a small dense world like the inner planets. It is definitely out of place.

(4) If we disregard Mercury and Venus, which are so close to the sun that gravitational effects have slowed them down, we can say that all the planets rotate rapidly about their axes. The periods of rotation range from 10 to 25 hours. Yet Pluto has a rotational period of 153 hours — nearly seven days.

Why all these extremes? Is there a reason for Pluto to be so different?

One particularly interesting suggestion has been made. Suppose Pluto wasn't a planet to begin with, but was a satellite of Neptune. Suppose some cosmic catastrophe of some sort had sent it hurtling out of its satellite orbit into an independent planetary one.

If so, the nature of the explosion (if that's what it was) could well have hurled it into a tilted and lopsided orbit, but one that brings it back toward Neptune, from where it had started out.

As a satellite, it would be small and perhaps dense, instead of being a gas giant like the true outer planets. And then, too, it would have rotated about its axis in the same time it took to revolve about Neptune, thanks to Neptune's gravitational pull. (This is true for satellites generally; it is true for our own moon.) In that case, Pluto's period of rotation could easily be a week. (Our moon's period of rotation is four weeks.) When Pluto was hurled away from Neptune, it may have kept its period of rotation and thus ended with a most peculiar one for a planet.

Unfortunately, though, all this is just speculation. There is no hard and fast evidence that Pluto was ever a satellite of Neptune; and if it was, we don't know what kind of catastrophe could have broken it away.

47

24

Why do comets have tails?

For many ages, comets have frightened mankind. Every once in a while, without apparent reason, a comet would appear in the sky. It had a shape unlike that of any other heavenly object. It was fuzzy rather than sharp-edged, and it had a dim tail streaming away from it. The tail looked like the disordered hair of a weeping woman to some imaginative people (the word "comet" is from the Latin for "hair") and it was thought to presage disaster.

In the eighteenth century, it was finally determined that some comets moved in regular orbits about the sun, but usually in very elongated ones. At the far end of their orbit they were invisible and it was only at the near end, which they approached once in dozens of years (or hundreds, or thousands), that they became visible.

In 1950, a Dutch astronomer, Jan H. Oort, suggested that there was a vast cloud of perhaps billions of planetoids circling the sun at a distance of a light-year or more. They would be over a thousand times as distant as Pluto, the farthest planet, and, despite their numbers, they would be completely invisible. Every once in a while, perhaps because of the gravitational pull of the nearer stars, some would find their orbital motions slowed and would begin to fall toward the sun. Occasionally, one would penetrate quite deeply into the inner solar system and would veer about the sun at a close approach of a few million miles. It would keep the new orbit thereafter and would be the kind of object we recognize as a comet.

About the same time, the American astronomer Fred L. Whipple suggested the comets were composed largely of low-boiling substances such as ammonia and methane, with grains of rocky material included.

In the comet cloud, far distant from the sun, the ammonia, methane, and other substances would be frozen into hard "ices."

The icy structure of the comets is stable in the outer fastnesses, but what happens when one of them slows up and falls much closer to the sun? As it enters the inner solar system, the increasing heat it receives from the sun causes its ices to begin to vaporize. The rocky particles trapped in the surface layer of ice are set free. The result is that the core of the comet is surrounded by a cloud of dust and vapor that thickens as it approaches the sun.

Emerging from the sun in every direction is the solar wind, an outward-streaming cloud of subatomic particles. The solar wind exerts a force that is greater than the comet's tiny gravitational attraction. The cloud of dust and vapor about the comet therefore begins to be pushed along by the solar wind and swept away from the sun. As the comet approaches the sun, the solar wind strengthens and the cloud of dust and vapor is pushed into a long tail stretching away from the sun. The closer the approach, the longer the tail, which is, however, composed of matter that is spread very very thin.

Naturally, comets don't last long once they enter the inner solar system. Each pass near the sun causes the loss of material, and, after a few dozen returns, the comets are reduced to a tiny rocky core or break up altogether into a cloud of small meteors. There are a number of "meteor streams" that move in regular orbits about the sun, and when some of them intersect the earth's atmosphere there is a gorgeous display of shooting stars. These are undoubtedly the remains of dead comets.

25

Why does the moon always keep the same side oriented toward the earth?

The gravitational attraction of the moon upon the earth raises the ocean on both sides of our planet, making two tidal bulges. As the earth rotates from west to east, these two tidal bulges, always facing toward the moon in one case and away from it in the other, move around the earth from east to west.

As the tidal bulges move around the earth, they scrape against the bottom of shallow seas such as the Bering Sea and the Irish Sea. This scraping sets up friction which converts energy of rotation into heat. Very slowly, as the earth's rotational energy is consumed in this manner, our planet's movement about its axis is slowed. The tides act as a brake on the earth's rotation and, in consequence, our days are getting one second longer every thousand years.

It isn't only the water of the ocean that lifts up in response to the moon's gravity. The solid crust of the earth also responds, though to a less noticeable extent. Two small bulges of rock circle the earth, one bulge facing toward the moon and the other on our planet's opposite side. As the bulges of rock move about the earth, the friction of rock layer against rock layer also bleeds the earth of its rotational energy. (The bulges don't move bodily about the planet, of course, but, as the planet turns, the bulge subsides in one place and forms in another, as different portions of the surface pass under the moon.)

The moon has no seas and no ordinary tides. However, the solid crust of the moon responds to the earth's gravitational force — and the earth's gravitational force is eighty times as large as that of the moon. The bulge drawn up from the moon's surface is much larger than the one drawn up on the earth's surface. The moon would therefore be subjected to considerably more tidal friction than we are, if it were rotating in a twenty-four-hour period. What's more, the moon, with a much smaller mass than earth's, would, for an equal period of rotation, have a far smaller total rotational energy to begin with.

As the moon's smaller initial supply of energy is bled off more rapidly by the large bulges formed by earth, its period of rotation would decrease at a comparatively rapid rate. Many millions of years ago it must have slowed to the point where the moon's day became equal to its month. Once that point was reached, the moon would always face one side to the earth.

That, in turn, freezes the bulges into position. One bulge would always face us in the very center of the side of the moon we see, and the other would point away from us in the very center of the side of the moon we don't see. Since those sides don't shift position as the moon revolves about us, there is no further motion of the bulges and no further frictional effect to alter the moon's rotational period. The moon will therefore continue to face one side toward us indefinitely — and, as you see, this is no coincidence, but an unavoidable effect of gravitation and friction.

The moon is a comparatively simple case. Under some circumstances, tidal friction can produce more complicated conditions of stability. For some eighty years, for instance, it was thought that Mercury (the closest planet to the sun and the one most strongly affected by the sun's gravity) kept one face to the sun for the same reason the moon keeps one face to the earth. Actually, it turns out that in the case of Mercury, frictional effects are able to produce a stable period of rotation of 58 days, which is just two-thirds as long as Mercury's 88-day period of revolution about the sun.

26

What are the mascons that have been discovered on the moon?

Newton's law of universal gravitation can be expressed as a very simple formula, provided all the objects in the universe are each supposed to have their mass concentrated at a single point. If the objects are very far away, we can suppose this is so, but the closer the objects are to each other, the more we have to take into account the fact that actually their mass is spread over a large body.

Even so, the treatment remains quite simple, provided 1) the object is a perfect sphere, and 2) its density is radially symmetrical. By "radially symmetrical" I mean that if an object is very dense at the center, and is less and less dense the farther from the center, the manner in which the density decreases is exactly the same no matter what direction we take from the center. Even if there are quite sudden changes in density, that doesn't matter, as long as these changes take place in just the same way in every possible direction from the center.

Astronomical objects almost fulfill these requirements if they are reasonably large. They are usually close to spherical in shape, and their density is almost radially symmetrical. Of course, we do have to allow for small deviations when objects are particularly close to each other. In studying the gravitational effects between the moon and the earth, we have to allow for the fact that the earth is not a perfect sphere but has an equatorial bulge. The extra matter in the bulge produces a tiny gravitational effect of its own that must be taken into account.

In the 1960s the United States put several space vehicles ("Lunar Orbiters") into orbit about the moon. Knowing the moon's size and shape in detail, our rocket experts were sure they could calculate exactly how quickly the vehicles would travel about the moon. To their surprise, however, they found that the vehicles moved just a trifle too quickly in some parts of the orbit.

The orbits were observed in detail, and it turned out that the vehicles speeded up very slightly when they passed over the large lunar "maria," the flat regions with few craters. This could only be because the moon was not quite radially symmetric in density. There must be extra mass concentrations in those maria which produced an additional gravitational effect that had not been allowed for. Astronomers began to speak of "mass concentrations" or, in abbreviated form, "mascons."

What are these mascons?

Two theories have arisen. Some astronomers think the maria are extra-huge craters produced by the collision of particularly large meteorites with the moon. These meteorites might have buried themselves under the surface of the maria and would still be there. They would be largely iron in composition, perhaps, and much denser than the moon's normal surface. They would thus represent an abnormally high concentration of mass.

A second theory is that during the moon's early history, the maria were really seas of water. Dense sediments were laid down before the water evaporated off into space and these would still be there, accounting for the extra concentration of mass.

Further exploration of the moon's surface ought to determine which of these theories (if either) is correct, and this might, in turn, tell us a great deal more about the moon's (and earth's) early history.

27

Now that we have landed on the moon six different times, what have we found out about it?

In a way, it is unfair to expect too much of our moon exploration, considering the limits of what we have done. After all, we have but scooped up some surface material from six widely separated places out of a total area equal to that of North and South America put together. On any one of their landings, astronauts might have been but five miles from some astonishing key to lunar puzzles and never have known it.

Then, too, astronomers and geologists are only at the start of their work. Studies of the moon rocks will continue for years. The process may well be useful, for some of the rocks are four billion years old or so and are relics of the first billion years of the existence of the solar system. Nothing on earth has ever been found that extends back, unchanged, to that early period.

Perhaps the clearest thing the investigation of the chemical makeup of the moon's surface has shown us is that the distribution of elements is significantly different from that on earth. Compared with earth, there is a shortage in the moon's surface rocks of those elements that tend to form low-melting compounds — such as hydrogen, carbon, sodium, lead, and so on. Those elements that form high-melting compounds, such as zirconium, titanium, and the rare earth metals, are present in greater percentage in the moon's crust than in our own.

A logical explanation for this is to suppose that the moon's surface was once heated quite strongly, and for a long enough period of time to cause the low-melting compounds to boil off and be lost, leaving the high-melting compounds behind untouched. This conclusion is further supported by the fact that there seems to be a large proportion of glassy materials on the moon, as though much of the surface had melted and then solidified again.

But what could have caused the heat? It might have been caused by the impact of large meteorites in the course of the early history of the moon, or large volcanic eruptions. If so, it might be that the effect would be found in some areas and not others. So far, though, the evidence seems to show the effect to be moonwide.

Perhaps it might have been caused by the fact that the sun went through a prolonged hot period at one time. If so, earth, too, would have been bathed in similar heat. While earth is protected by air and ocean as the moon is not, there might be some evidence on earth of this period of heat. None has been found, but perhaps that is because there are no rocks on earth that have existed unchanged from that first billion years of the solar system.

A third possibility is that the moon was once considerably closer to the sun than it now is. It may originally have been an independent planet with an elongated orbit that, at one end, brought it about as close to the sun as Mercury is. In that case, its surface would have been thoroughly sun-baked.

The other end of its orbit may have brought it moderately close to earth's orbit, and perhaps at some time in the past, even as recently as a billion years ago, the situation was such that earth managed to capture it, and what had been a planet became a satellite.

Whatever the cause, that baked surface of the moon is disheartening in one respect. It increases the possibility that there is no water anywhere in the upper few miles of the moon's surface, and that means that establishing a moon colony will be much harder than it otherwise might have been.

28

Is there life on Mars?

We really don't know yet. We may never know unless we actually land scientists on Mars and let them investigate.

From what we can tell so far, though, things look hopeful for Martian life. To be sure, the Mars probe *Mariner IX,* placed in orbit about a thousand miles above the surface of Mars, observed no signs of life though the whole planet was mapped. However, if earth were viewed from the same distance in the same way, no signs of life would be seen there either.

Mars's atmosphere is very thin, only 1/100 as dense as earth's, and what there is of it is almost entirely carbon dioxide. Then, too, Mars is half again as far from the sun as we are, so that temperatures drop to Antarctic figures at night and in the polar regions it is cold enough to freeze carbon dioxide.

Men couldn't survive in such an environment without special protection. In fact, no earthly animals could. Earthmen colonizing Mars would have to live under domes, or in caverns underground. But does this mean that complex life-forms might not exist on Mars that are adapted to Martian conditions? The chances are very small, perhaps, but we can't absolutely eliminate the possibility.

What about simple life-forms — lichenlike plants or bacterialike microorganisms? The chances are far better in that case. Perhaps even fairly good.

Admittedly there was some hope that simple life-forms might exist on the moon and that went glimmering, but Mars offers a much more favorable environment than the moon does. Mars is farther from the sun than the moon is and has an atmosphere that offers a little protection, so Mars is less subjected to the sun's hard radiation which would break up the complicated molecules necessary to life.

Next, Mars, being colder and larger than the moon, is more successful in retaining the volatile substances that serve as the fundamental starting points for life. Mars is rich in carbon dioxide and undoubtedly has water. Out of these, life can form. If, as it turns out, some forms of very simple earth life can continue to live under simulated Martian conditions, how much more that would be true of life-forms adapted to Martian conditions to begin with.

The *Mariner IX* photographs show that Martian conditions need not always be as severe as they are now. There are volcanic regions on Mars, with one giant volcano, Nix Olympica, twice as broad as any earthly volcano. This means that Mars is an active world geologically and is undergoing changes.

There are winding markings on Mars that look for all the world like riverbeds, and some astronomers even speculate that their appearance shows that water was flowing through them not very long ago, geologically speaking. What's more, the polar ice caps on Mars look as though they go through alternate periods of growth and recession.

Perhaps Mars alternates through a kind of long winter, in which almost the entire atmosphere is frozen and what is left is very thin (as is true now); and a kind of long summer, in which almost the entire atmosphere thaws out and is then almost as thick as earth's.

It may be that life-forms now lie dormant in Mars's soil and that when the long summer comes, and the atmosphere thickens and water flows, life may flourish to an extent greater than we might now expect.

29

Suppose there is simple life on Mars. Is it really worth going all the way out there just to look at it?

Scientists wouldn't hesitate for a second to answer that with the strongest possible "Yes!"

All forms of earth life, without exception, are based on the large molecules of proteins and nucleic acids. All use the same sort of chemical reactions mediated by the same sort of enzymes. All earth life consists of variations on a single theme.

If there is life on Mars, however simple, it may exist as variations on *another* theme. At one stroke we would double the kinds of life we know and perhaps gain, immediately, a more fundamental understanding of the nature of life.

Even if life on Mars proves to be based on the same theme as earth life, there may be interesting differences in detail. For instance, all protein molecules on earth are built up of amino acids, and these (all but one) are capable of either a left-handed or a right-handed orientation. Under all conditions not involving life, the two types are equally stable and exist in equal quantities.

In earthly proteins, however, all the amino acids, with only the most insignificant and rare exceptions, are left-handed. This means protein molecules can be built up in neat stacks, which would be impossible if some were left-handed and some were right-handed. The stacks would be just as neat if all were right-handed, however.

Why left-handed and not right-handed then? Is it a matter of chance? Did the first blob of life on earth just happen to be left-handed? Or is there some basic asymmetry in nature that makes the left-handed form inevitable? Mars life might answer this question and others like it.

Even if Martian life turned out to be based on the same theme as earthly life and to be identical in every detail, it would be worth learning this fact. The fact might serve as interesting evidence to the effect that the life theme as it exists on earth might be the only one possible on any planet that is even vaguely earthlike.

Besides, if Mars life were a carbon copy of earth life, biochemically speaking, the former might still be made up of molecular systems more primitive than anything that has developed over the eons in the lusher and softer surroundings on earth. In that case, Mars would be a laboratory in which we could observe protolife like that which once (perhaps) existed on earth. We might even experiment with it — as on earth we could do only if we owned a time machine — and probe for some fundamental truths that are hidden in the complexities of earthly life.

Indeed, even if life did not exist on Mars at all, there might well be organic molecules in the soil which, though nonliving, might be clearly on the way, so to speak, to life. They might indicate the nature of the path once taken on earth during the period of "chemical evolution" before the development of the first system complex enough to be called living.

Whatever we learn on Mars concerning life will, very likely, help us understand our own earth life a little more clearly (just as the study of Latin and French helps us understand English a little more clearly). And, surely, if we go to Mars in order to learn more about earth than we can learn on earth itself, that is reason enough to try to do it if we can.

30

How and when were the oceans formed?

In the early part of the twentieth century, it was thought that the earth and the other planets were formed of matter pulled out of the sun. We had the picture of an earth gradually cooling down from white heat, to red heat, to mere hotness, and finally to the boiling point of water. When it had gotten cool enough for water to condense, the water vapor in earth's heated atmosphere did so and it began to rain and rain — and rain. After many years of an incredible rain of boiling water that fizzed and sputtered as it struck the hot earth, the hollows of the planet's rough surface finally cooled enough to hold the water and filled up to form our oceans.

Very dramatic — but almost certainly completely wrong.

Currently, scientists are convinced the earth and the other planets did not form from the sun, but were formed of particles coming together at the same time that the sun itself was being formed. The earth was never at sun temperature, but it did grow quite warm through the energies of collision of all the particles that formed it. It grew warm enough so that its relatively small mass could not hold an atmosphere or water vapor to begin with.

The solid body of the newly formed earth had, in other words, neither atmosphere nor ocean. Where, then, did they come from?

There existed water (and gases) in loose combination with the rocky substances making up the solid portion of the globe. As that solid portion packed together more and more tightly under the pull of gravity, its interior grew hotter and hotter. Water vapor and gas were forced out of combination with the rock and came fizzing from its substance.

The gaseous bubbles, forming and collecting, racked the baby earth

with enormous quakes; escaping heat produced violent volcanic eruptions. For unnumbered years, liquid water did *not* fall from the sky; rather, water vapor whistled out of the crust and then condensed. The oceans formed from below, not from above.

What geologists mainly dispute now is the rate at which the oceans formed. Did the water vapor all fizz out within a billion years or less, so that the ocean has been its present size ever since life began? Or has the process been so slow that the ocean has been growing all through geologic time and is still growing?

Those who maintain the ocean formed early in the game and has been steady in size for a long time point out that the continents seem to be a permanent feature of the earth. They do not appear to have been much larger in the past, when the ocean was, supposedly, much smaller.

On the other hand, those who maintain the ocean has been growing steadily point out that volcanic eruptions even today pour quantities of water vapor into the air; water vapor derived from deep-lying rocks, not from the ocean. Also, there are sea mounts under the Pacific with flat tops that may have once been at ocean level but are now hundreds of feet below.

A compromise may be possible. It is suggested that the ocean has indeed been growing steadily, but that, as the quantity of water increased, its weight forced the ocean bed downward. In short, the oceans have been growing steadily deeper, not broader. This would account for both the drowned sea mounts and the nondrowned continents.

31

Are the oceans growing saltier? Will they
ever become salty enough to kill all life?

There is a water cycle that exists on earth. About 30,000 cubic miles
of water are evaporated from the ocean each year. This falls as rain
and, one way or another, returns to the ocean.

The two branches of the cycle, evaporation and return, are not balanced in one way. Of the contents of the ocean, only water itself is
evaporated so that rain is almost pure water. Some of the water that
returns, however, hits land first, trickles through soil, and picks up some
soluble chemicals which it carries down to the ocean along with itself.
River water, for instance, is about 1/100 of 1 percent salt — not enough
to taste, but enough to be important.

It would seem, then, that the ocean is constantly gaining traces of
salt and other chemicals from the land, but loses none through evaporation. We might argue that the ocean must be growing saltier and
saltier; very slowly, of course, but over the millions of years of geologic
time, the salt should pile up enormously. Right now, for instance, the
ocean contains about 3.5 percent dissolved material, most of which is
ordinary salt.

River water also brings its salt into some inland lakes which have no
connection with the ocean. There the dissolved material accumulates
as it does in the ocean. If the lake is in a hot area, so that its average
rate of evaporation is greater than that of the ocean, the dissolved
material accumulates more rapidly and it can become far saltier than
the ocean. The Dead Sea, on the border of Israel and Jordan, is 25
percent dissolved matter. It is so salty that nothing can live in it.

Is the ocean headed for this dead end, too, eventually?

It might be so if there weren't processes which tend to reduce the salt content of the ocean. Storms, for instance, blow spray far inland and dissolved salts are carried with the spray to be distributed over the land.

To a much more important extent, certain combinations of dissolved substances, when present in sufficient concentration, combine to form insoluble compounds that sink to the bottom of the ocean. Other substances, though not insoluble in themselves, can combine with the material on the ocean floor. Then, too, certain substances are absorbed into the cells of ocean organisms.

The result is that the ocean is far less rich in dissolved matter than it ought to be if we calculate all the material that must have been brought into it by rivers over the past few billion years. On the other hand, the ocean floor is quite rich in substances that must have come from land. Large quantities of metals lie in nodules distributed over the ocean floor.

Then, too, in the course of time shallow arms of the ocean may be pinched off by rising bits of land. These bits of ocean gradually evaporate, leaving behind large quantities of dissolved material that have in this way been returned to land. Salt mines, from which one can obtain vast quantities of salt and lesser quantities of other substances, are the leftover remnants of such dried-up bits of ocean.

Well, then, what is the overall result? Is the ocean getting very slightly saltier in the long run? Is it actually getting less salty? Does it sometimes veer in one direction, sometimes in the other, keeping a balance on the average? Geologists don't really know.

32

Is there really gold in the ocean?

Yes, indeed. Why not?

Rainwater is constantly trickling over the dry land on its way back to the ocean and, in the process of doing so, it dissolves a little bit of all the materials it soaks up and pours past. Not much is dissolved altogether and some substances are less soluble than others; and after the dissolved substances reach the ocean, some make their way to the sea bottom.

Nevertheless, in the billions of years that the ocean has existed, so much dissolved material has been dumped into it that there are vast quantities of every element in the compounds that are mixed with the water molecules of the sea.

About 3.25 percent of the sea is dissolved solid matter; and there are 330,000,000 cubic miles of ocean water, all told, weighing 1½ billion billion tons. If all the solid matter were separated out of the seawater, it would come to a total weight of 50 million billion (50,000,000,000,-000,000) tons. Over three fourths of the solid matter is, of course, ordinary salt, but a little bit of everything is in the remaining fourth.

For instance, there are enough magnesium compounds present to yield a total of 19 hundred thousand billion (1,900,000,000,000,000) tons of that metal. Such a supply in the ocean is enough to last us an enormous length of time, especially since whatever we extract and use eventually gets washed back into the ocean.

The magnesium isn't spread out unevenly, however, with rich pockets here and there (as minerals on land are). It is spread evenly throughout the ocean, which means that even if we worked with perfect efficiency, we would have to extract the magnesium from 95 gallons of seawater to get a pound of it. Methods have been worked out to do this economically, and magnesium is now profitably obtained from seawater in almost any necessary quantity.

Another element present in sizable quantities in seawater is bromine (a relative of chlorine, but less common). The sea contains dissolved compounds that would yield a total of a hundred thousand billion (100,000,000,000,000) tons of bromine. This is about a twentieth of the supply of magnesium, so twenty times as much seawater — about 1850 gallons — must be scoured of its contents (at perfect efficiency) to get a pound of bromine. This, too, can be done profitably, and the sea is a major supplier of the world's bromine.

A third relative of chlorine and bromine is iodine. This is a rarer element than either, in the world at large, and it is present in the ocean to less than a thousandth of the quantity of bromine. The total amounts to 86 billion tons, which still sounds like a lot, but this means that there is only one pound of it in 2 million gallons of seawater. This is too little to be profitably extracted directly. Fortunately seaweed extracts the iodine for us, and important quantities of iodine can be obtained commercially from seaweed ash.

Which brings us to gold. The total quantity of gold in seawater is somewhere between 6 and 12 million tons. If this figure had been given at the start of the article it would have sounded like a great deal. At least 6 million *tons!* Maybe twice as much. Wow!

By now, though, you can see that isn't much. Since 13 to 27 billion gallons (or 25 to 50 cubic miles) of ocean would have to be ransacked to extract a single pound of gold, it would cost far more than a pound of gold to do it. So the gold is just left in the ocean.

33

What would happen if the ice caps melted?

The earth's land areas carry a load of nearly 9 million cubic miles of ice (about 85 percent of it on the continent of Antarctica). Since water is somewhat denser than ice, this load of ice would melt down to about 8 million cubic miles of water.

Naturally, if the ice melted, almost all that water would run off the land areas into the ocean. The ocean has a total surface area of 140 million square miles. If that surface area remained constant and the 8 million cubic miles of melted ice were to spread out evenly over the top of the ocean, it would be 8/140 or 0.057 miles thick. This means that the layer of melted ice would be 300 feet thick.

However, the surface area of the ocean would not remain constant, for if its level rose it would spill out over a couple of million square miles of the low-lying land areas along its shores. This means the ocean's surface area would increase and the layer of new water would not be as thick as we have just supposed. Furthermore, the added weight of water would depress the ocean bottom somewhat. Still, the ocean level would probably rise 200 feet, enough to reach the twentieth story of the Empire State Building and to drown much of earth's most densely populated areas.

Throughout earth's geologic history, the quantity of land ice has varied considerably. During the height of an ice age, mile-high glaciers advance over millions of square miles of land and the water level of the ocean drops so much that the continental shelves are exposed as dry land.

On the other hand, when the ice load is virtually zero, as it has been for tens of millions of years at a time, the ocean level is high and the continental area small.

Neither situation is necessarily catastrophic. At the height of an ice age, millions of square miles of land are covered by ice and are uninhabitable to land life. On the other hand, millions of square miles of continental shelves are exposed and habitable.

If, contrariwise, the ice is gone, millions of square miles of land are covered by water and are uninhabitable to land life. On the other hand, without ice, and with smaller land areas, the climate is more equable and there are few deserts, so that a larger percentage of what land surface is left is habitable. And the change in total ocean volume is comparatively small (6 or 7 percent at most) so sea life is not much affected.

If the change in sea level were to take place over thousands and tens of thousands of years, as it always has in the past, man could well cope with the change. The difficulty is, however, that man's technology is pouring dust and carbon dioxide into the air. The dust tends to cut off solar radiation and cool the earth, while the carbon dioxide tends to trap heat and warm the earth. If one effect predominates much over the other in times to come, earth's temperature may fall or rise comparatively rapidly. Continental glaciers may form or the ice cap may melt in a matter of 100 years or so.

It will then be the rapidity of the change, not so much the change itself, that will be catastrophic.

34

Where did the air we breathe come from?

The planets originated, astronomers suspect, out of swirls of gas and dust made up, in general, of the various elements present in their usual cosmic abundance. About 90 percent of the atoms were hydrogen and another 9 percent were helium. The rest included all the other elements — mainly neon, oxygen, carbon, nitrogen, argon, sulfur, silicon, magnesium, iron, and aluminum.

The solid globe of the earth itself formed out of a rocky mixture of magnesium, iron, and aluminum silicates and sulfides, with molecules that clung tightly together through chemical forces. Excess iron slowly sank through the rock to form a hot, metallic core.

The solid matter of the earth, as it collected, trapped some gaseous material and retained it in spaces between solid particles or through loose chemical union. These gases would include atoms of helium, neon, and argon, which remained uncombined; and atoms of hydrogen, which either combined in pairs among themselves to form hydrogen molecules (H_2), or combined with other atoms. They could combine with oxygen to form water (H_2O), with nitrogen to form ammonia (NH_3), or with carbon to form methane (CH_4).

As the material of the forming earth packed down, gases fizzed out through the squeezing effect of pressure and the more violent effect of volcanic action. Molecules of hydrogen, as well as atoms of helium and neon, are too light to be retained and they escaped rapidly.

Earth's atmosphere came to be made up of what remained: water vapor, ammonia, methane plus a little argon. Most, but not all, of the water vapor condensed to form an ocean.

This is still the sort of atmosphere possessed by planets such as Jupiter and Saturn, which, however, are large enough to retain hydrogen, helium, and neon.

The atmosphere of the inner planets, however, began to evolve chemically. The ultraviolet rays from the nearby sun broke up molecules of water vapor to hydrogen and oxygen. The hydrogen escaped, but the oxygen accumulated and combined with ammonia and methane. With ammonia, the oxygen combined to form nitrogen and water; with methane, to form carbon dioxide and water. Gradually, the atmosphere of the inner planets changed from ammonia plus methane to nitrogen plus carbon dioxide. Mars and Venus have nitrogen plus carbon dioxide atmospheres today, and the earth must have had such an atmosphere at the time life first formed billions of years ago.

Moreover, such an atmosphere is stable. Once it is formed, additional ultraviolet action on water vapor allows free oxygen (with molecules made up of two oxygen atoms, O_2) to accumulate. Further ultraviolet action alters such oxygen to ozone (with three oxygen atoms to the molecule, O_3). Ozone absorbs ultraviolet and cuts it off. Little ultraviolet can penetrate the ozone layer in the upper atmosphere to break up water molecules below and the chemical evolution of the atmosphere stops — until such time as something new is added.

On earth, something new *was* added. A group of life-forms happened to develop that could use *visible* light to break up water molecules. Visible light was not stopped by the ozone layer and the process (photosynthesis) could go on indefinitely. Through photosynthesis, carbon dioxide was consumed and oxygen was released. Beginning about half a billion years ago, then, the atmosphere was converted to the nitrogen plus oxygen one we have today.

35

What is the greenhouse effect?

When we say that some object is "transparent" because we can see through it, we don't necessarily mean that all kinds of light can pass through it. For instance, we can see through red glass, which is therefore transparent, but blue light won't go through it. Ordinary glass is transparent to all colors of light; it is, however, only slightly transparent to ultraviolet or infrared radiation.

Now imagine a glass house standing out in the sunlight. The visible light of the sun passes right through the glass and is absorbed by whatever is present inside the house. The objects in the house warm up as a result, just as do objects outside the house exposed to the direct light of the sun.

Objects warmed by sunlight give off that warmth again in the form of radiation. They are not at the temperature of the sun, however, so they don't give off energetic visible light. They give off, instead, the much less energetic infrared radiation. After a while, they give off as much energy in the form of infrared as they absorb in the form of sunlight, and their temperature remains constant (though they are warmer, of course, than they would be if the sun weren't shining on them).

Objects in the open have little trouble getting rid of their infrared radiation, but the sun-warmed objects inside the glass house are in another situation altogether. Only small quantities of the infrared radiation they give off will go through the glass. Most is reflected, so that energy accumulates within. The temperature of the objects inside the house rises considerably higher than does the temperature of the objects outside. The temperature inside rises until enough infrared radiation can leak through the glass to set up an equilibrium.

Because of this, plants can be grown inside a glass house even though

the temperature outside the house is cold enough to freeze them. The flourishing greenery inside such a glass house gives it the name of a "greenhouse." The additional warmth inside the greenhouse caused by the fact that glass is quite transparent to visible light and only slightly transparent to infrared is called the "greenhouse effect."

Our atmosphere consists almost entirely of oxygen, nitrogen, and argon. These gases are quite transparent to both visible light and to the kind of infrared radiation the earth's surface gives off when it is warmed. The atmosphere also contains 0.03 percent of carbon dioxide, however, and this is transparent to visible light but not very transparent to infrared. The carbon dioxide of the atmosphere acts like the glass of the greenhouse.

Because carbon dioxide is present in such small quantities in our atmosphere, the effect is comparatively minor. Even so, the earth is a bit warmer than it would be if there were no carbon dioxide present at all. What's more, if the carbon dioxide content of the atmosphere were to double, the increased greenhouse effect would warm the earth a couple of additional degrees and that would be enough to bring about a gradual melting of the ice caps at the poles.

An example of an enormous greenhouse effect is to be found on Venus, where the very thick atmosphere seems to be mostly carbon dioxide. Astronomers expected Venus to be warmer than the earth since it is considerably closer to the sun. Not knowing the details of the composition of its atmosphere, they had not expected the additional warming of the greenhouse effect. They were quite surprised when they found that Venus's surface temperature was far above the boiling point of water and hundreds of degrees warmer than they had expected.

36

What happens to planetary probes after they have passed a planet? Where do they go?

Most satellites sent up by the U.S.A. and the U.S.S.R. have been placed in orbit about the earth.

A satellite's orbit may, of course, intersect the earth's surface so that it returns to the planet after a single looping upward thrust. The first two "suborbital" flights of the Mercury capsules were of this type. Sometimes a satellite's orbit makes such a large loop around the earth that it gets beyond the moon as well, as *Lunik III* did in taking pictures of the moon's "other side."

If a satellite is sent upward at velocities of more than 7 miles per second, it will not be held by the earth's gravitational field, but will move into an independent orbit about the sun, which has a stronger gravitational field than earth has and which can hold the faster-moving bodies. An around-the-sun orbit may intersect the surface of some heavenly body, as in the case of *Rangers VII, VIII,* and *IX,* which crashed into the moon (on purpose, of course).

A satellite in orbit about the sun may not intersect the surface of any heavenly body, and it would then keep to its ellipse about the sun indefinitely. The various "lunar probes" and "planetary probes" are of this variety.

Probes sent into orbit about the sun can have their courses adjusted so that in the course of their first revolution they will make a close approach to the moon (*Pioneer IV*), to Venus (*Mariner II*), or to Mars (*Mariner IV*). In the course of this approach, the probe will send back information concerning the body it passes and the space surrounding it. The probe will then move past the heavenly body and continue on its orbit about the sun.

If the probes weren't affected by the gravitational field of the planet they passed, they would eventually return to the point in space from which they were launched (but the earth would have moved on in its orbit in the meantime and would no longer be there).

As it is, however, the planetary probe moves into a new orbit as a result of the pull of the planet it passes. Indeed, its orbit shifts somewhat every time it passes fairly close to some massive body, so that it is just about impossible to predict exactly where a particular probe will be after a revolution or two about the sun. The equations representing their motions are entirely too complicated to be worth the bother of trying to solve.

Of course, if probes could continue to broadcast a signal they could be followed whatever their orbit — especially when close to the earth.

Once the batteries on a probe die, however, the satellites are lost. They can't signal, and they are too small to see. All probes are eventually lost and that is to be expected.

They continue to follow orbits about the sun, however, and remain in the same general regions of space. They do not wander off on long voyages to other planets. Since we receive no information from them, they are useless and can only be chalked off as "interplanetary garbage." If they don't blunder into the earth, moon, Mars, or Venus in some future revolution about the sun, they may well move on forever in orbit.

37

How will the earth end?

The first to attempt a detailed study of the history of the earth, past and possible future, without reference to divine intervention was the Scottish geologist James Hutton. In 1785, he published the first book of modern geology and had to admit that, from studying the earth itself, he could see no signs of a beginning and no prospect of an end.

We have gone further since. We are pretty certain that the earth attained its present shape about 4.7 billion years ago. It was about then that, out of the dust and gas of the original nebula that formed the solar system, the earth as we know it came into being. Once formed, the earth, *if left to itself* as a collection of metal and rock covered by a thin film of water and air, would exist, as far as we can tell, forever.

But will it be left to itself?

The nearest object that is large enough and possesses energy enough to affect the earth seriously is the sun. As long as the sun maintains its present level of activity (which it has done for billions of years), the earth will continue essentially unchanged. But can the sun continue to maintain that level? And if it doesn't, what change will take place, and how will that change affect the earth?

Until the 1930s it seemed obvious that the sun, like any other hot object, would simply have to cool down. It kept pouring energy into space and, as it kept doing so, that immense flood would slow down and gradually be reduced to a trickle. As this happened, the sun would cool to orange, then red, grow dimmer and dimmer, and finally flicker out.

Under those conditions the earth would slowly cool, too. More and more of its water would freeze; the polar areas would expand. Eventually, even the equatorial regions would lack warmth enough to sustain life. The entire ocean would freeze into a solid block of ice; the very air would liquefy and freeze. For uncounted trillions of years thereafter, the frozen earth (and its fellow planets) would circle the dead sun.

But under those conditions, the earth as a planet would still exist.

In the 1930s, however, nuclear scientists began to work out for the first time the nuclear reactions that went on within the sun and other stars. They found that though the sun must cool eventually, there would be periods of strong heating preceding that end. Once most of the basic hydrogen fuel is consumed, other nuclear reactions will take place that will heat the sun and cause it to expand enormously. Though it will give off more total heat, each bit of its now vast surface will have a much smaller fraction of that heat and will be cooler. The sun will become a red giant.

Under those conditions, it is likely that the earth will be first heated to a cinder and, eventually, vaporized. In that case, the earth will really come to an end as a solid planetary body. But don't worry too much about it yet. Figure about 8 billion years.

38

What is a theoretical physicist and what sort of work does he do?

The science of physics deals primarily with energy in its various forms and with the interaction of energy with matter. A physicist would be interested in the laws governing motion, since any piece of matter in motion would possess "kinetic energy." He would be interested in heat, sound, light, electricity, magnetism, and radioactivity, for all represent forms of energy. In the twentieth century, it even became apparent that mass is a form of energy.

A physicist would also be interested in the manner in which one form of energy is converted into another and in the rules governing that conversion.

Naturally, physicists can specialize. If one of them is particularly interested in the interaction of energy and subatomic particles, he is a "nuclear physicist." (The nucleus is the chief structure within the atom.) If he is interested in the interaction of energy and matter in stars, he is an "astrophysicist" (the Greek word "aster" means "star").

Then, too, someone who is particularly interested in the energy aspects of chemical reactions is a "physical chemist" and someone who is chiefly interested in the manner in which living tissue handles and produces energy is a "biophysicist" (the Greek word "bios" means "life").

A physicist may be absorbed in making careful measurements under various controlled conditions. He may want to measure the exact amount of heat produced by certain chemical reactions. He may want to measure the exact manner in which a particular subatomic particle breaks down to liberate other particles plus energy. He may want to measure the exact manner in which tiny electric potentials in the brain vary under the influence of certain drugs. In all these cases, he is essentially an "experimental physicist."

On the other hand, a physicist may be particularly interested in studying careful measurements which have already been obtained, in order to see if he can make general sense out of them. Perhaps he can figure out some mathematical relationship which would explain why all those measurements are what they are. If he works out such a mathematical relationship, he can use it to predict the values of other measurements that have not yet been made. If these measurements, once made, turn out to be as predicted, he may well have advanced something that is often called a "law of nature."

Physicists who try to work out laws of nature in this way are "theoretical physicists."

There are some superbly gifted experimental physicists who are not particularly interested in theorizing. Albert A. Michelson, who invented the interferometer and made accurate measurements of the speed of light, is an example. There are also superbly gifted theoretical physicists who are not at all interested in experimenting. Albert Einstein, the founder of the theory of relativity, was one of those.

Both experimental and theoretical physicists are extremely valuable to science, even if the former restrict themselves to measurement and the latter to mathematical reasoning. It is always fascinating, however, to find someone who is first-class both as an experimenter and as a theoretician. Enrico Fermi was an outstanding example of such a "double-threat" physicist. (He was also an outstanding teacher, which made him, perhaps, "triple-threat.")

39

Is time an illusion or does it really
exist? How would you describe it?

Time, to begin with, is a psychological matter; it is a sense of duration. You eat and then, after a while, you are hungry again. It is day, then, after a while, it is night.

What this sense of duration is, what it is that makes you aware of something happening "after a while," is part of the problem of the mechanism of the mind generally — a problem yet to be solved.

Each individual comes to realize that his sensation of duration varies with circumstances. A day at work seems much longer than a day with your sweetheart; an hour at a dull lecture seems longer than an hour at cards. This might mean that what we call a "day" or an "hour" is longer at some times than at others, but there is a catch. A period of duration that seems short to one may seem long to another, and neither unusually long nor short to a third.

If the sense of duration is to be useful to a group of people, some method of measuring its length must be found that is universal and not personal. If a group agrees to meet "in exactly six weeks," it would be useless to have each individual appear at the meeting place when he feels somewhere inside himself that six weeks have passed. Instead, all must agree to count forty-two periods of light-darkness and then show up regardless of what his sense of duration tells him.

When we choose some objective physical phenomenon as a means of substituting counting for our innate sense of duration, we have something we can refer to as "time." In that sense, we mustn't try to define time as something, but merely as a system of measurement.

The first measurements of time involved periodic astronomic phenomena: the repetition of noon (sun at maximum height) marked off the day; the repetition of the new moon marked off the month; the repetition of vernal equinox (the noon-day sun over the equator after

the cold season) marked off the year. By dividing the day into equal smaller units we get hours, minutes, and seconds.

These small units of time could not be measured accurately, however, until use was made of a periodic motion more rapid than the repetition of noon. The use of the even swinging of a pendulum and of the even oscillation of a hairspring made modern timepieces possible in the seventeenth century. Only then did the measurement of time become reasonably precise. Nowadays, we use the vibrations of atoms for even greater precision.

How can we be sure that these periodic phenomena are really "even"? Might they not be as unreliable as our sense of duration?

Maybe so, but there are several independent ways of measuring time and we can compare them with one another. If any of them are markedly uneven, this will show up in comparison to the others. If *all* the ways are uneven, then it is enormously unlikely that they will all be uneven in exactly the same fashion. If, then, the methods of measuring time match very closely, *as they do,* we can only conclude that the various periodic phenomena we use are all essentially even! (Not perfectly even, though. The day length varies very slightly, for instance.)

Physical measurements measure "physical time." Various organisms, including man, have methods of involving themselves in periodic phenomena (such as waking and sleeping) even without reference to outside changes (like day and night). Such "biological time" is not as remorselessly even as physical time, however.

And, of course, there is the sense of duration or "psychological time." Even with a clock in plain view, it *still* seems that a day at work lasts longer than a day with your sweetheart.

40

What is the smallest possible unit of time?

Shortly after 1800, it was suggested that matter came in certain small units called "atoms." Shortly after 1900, it was accepted that energy came in certain small units called "quanta." Well, then, is there any other commonly measured quantity that comes in small fixed units? Does time, for instance?

There are two ways of finding a "smallest possible unit." There is the direct way of dividing some measured quantity until it can be divided no more — to break down measured masses into smaller and smaller quantities till you have a single atom, or to break down measured energies till you have a single quantum. The other is the indirect way of noting some phenomenon that can't be explained unless you *assume* the existence of a smaller possible unit.

In the case of matter, a wide variety of chemical observations, including the "law of definite proportions" and the "law of multiple proportions," made an atomic theory necessary. In the case of energy, a consideration of the radiation of a black body and of the existence of a photoelectric effect made a quantum theory necessary.

In the case of time, the indirect method fails — at least so far. There are no observed phenomena that make it necessary to suppose that there is a smallest possible unit of time.

What about the direct method? Can we observe shorter and shorter periods of time until we come to something that is ultimately short?

Physicists began to deal with ultrashort time intervals after the discovery of radioactivity. Some types of atoms had a very short half-life. Polonium-212, for instance, has a half-life of less than a millionth (10^{-6}) of a second. It decayed in the time it took the earth to travel one inch in its 18½-mile-per-second journey about the sun. Yet, though physicists studied these processes in detail, there was no sign, during that interval, of a time flow in little bits rather than continuously.

But we can go farther. Some subatomic particles break down in far shorter intervals of time. In a bubble chamber, certain particles, traveling at nearly the speed of light, manage to form tracks three centimeters long after forming and before breaking down. This corresponds to a lifetime of a ten-billionth (10^{-10}) of a second.

Even that is not the best we can do. In the 1960s, particularly short-lived particles were discovered. They existed so briefly that, even traveling at nearly the speed of light, they could not move far enough to leave a measurable track. The length of time they existed had to be calculated by indirect methods and it turned out that these ultra-short-lived "resonance particles" existed for only ten trillionths of a trillionth (10^{-23}) of a second.

Such a short time is impossible to grasp. A resonance particle's lifetime is to a millionth of a second as a millionth of a second is to 3000 years.

Or look at it another way. Light travels in a vacuum at nearly 300,000 kilometers a second and this is the fastest known velocity. How far can light travel while a resonance particle comes into being and goes out of being? The answer is 10^{-13} centimeters or just about the width of a proton!

Yet there is no reason to think the lifetime of a resonance particle must be the smallest bit of time there can be. There is still no sign of a limit.

41

What is the fourth dimension?

The word "dimension" is from Latin and means "to measure completely." Let's try a few measurements, then.

Suppose you have a line and want to locate a fixed point, X, on it in such a way that someone else can find that point from your description. You make a mark anywhere on the line, to begin with, and label it "zero." You then make a measurement and find that X is just two inches from the zero mark. If it is on one side, you agree to call the distance +2; if on the other side, it is −2.

Your point is located, then, with a single number, provided everyone agrees on the "conventions" — where the zero mark is, and which side is plus, which side minus.

Since only one number is needed to locate a point on a line, the line, or any piece of it, is "one-dimensional" ("one number to measure completely").

Suppose, though, you had a large sheet of paper and wanted to locate a fixed point, X, on it. You begin from your zero mark and find it is 5 inches away — but in which direction? You can break it down into two directions. It is 3 inches north and 4 inches east. If you call north plus and south minus, and if you call east plus and west minus, you can locate the point with two numbers: +3, +4.

Or you could say it was 5 inches from the zero mark at an angle of 36.87° from the east-west line. Here again are two numbers: 5 and 36.87°. No matter how you do it, you must have two numbers to locate a fixed point on a plane. A plane or any piece of it is two-dimensional.

Suppose now that you have a space like the inside of a room. A fixed point, X, could be located as 5 inches north of a certain zero mark, 2 inches east of it, and 15 inches *above* it. Or you can locate it by giving one distance and two angles. However you slice it, you will need three numbers to locate a fixed point in the inside of a room (or in the inside of the universe).

The room, or the universe, is therefore three-dimensional.

Suppose there were a space of such a nature that four numbers, or five, or eighteen, are absolutely required to locate a fixed point in it. That would be four-dimensional space, or five-dimensional space, or eighteen-dimensional space. Such spaces don't exist in the ordinary universe, but mathematicians can imagine such "hyperspaces" and work out what the properties of mathematical figures in such spaces would be. They even work out the properties of figures that would hold true for any dimensional space. This is "n-dimensional geometry."

But what if you are dealing with points that aren't fixed, but that change position with time? If you wanted to locate a mosquito flying about a room, you would give the usual three numbers: north-south, east-west, and up-down. *Then* you would have to add a fourth number representing the time, because the mosquito would have been in that spatial position for only a particular instant, and that instant you must identify.

This is true for everything in the universe. You have space, which is three-dimensional, and you must add time to produce a four-dimensional "space-time." However, time must be treated differently from the three "spatial dimensions." In certain key equations where the symbols for the three spatial dimensions have a positive sign, the symbol for time must have a negative one.

So we mustn't say that time is *the* fourth dimension. It is merely *a* fourth dimension, and different from the other three.

42

What is meant by curved space?

On first encountering the notion that Einstein's theory of relativity speaks of "curved space," one has a right, perhaps, to feel puzzled. How can the vacuum of space be curved? How can you bend emptiness?

To see how that might be, let's begin by imagining someone in a spaceship carefully watching a nearby planet. The planet is covered completely by a deep ocean, so that it is a sphere with a surface as smooth as a polished billiard ball. Let us suppose there is a ship sailing over the planetary ocean, along the equator, due east.

Now let's imagine something more. The planet is completely invisible to the observer. All he can see is the ship. As he studies its line of motion, he finds to his surprise that the ship is following a circular path. Eventually, it will return to its starting point and it will then have marked out a complete circle.

If the ship changes its course, the line bends and is no longer a simple circle. However, no matter how the ship changes its course, no matter how it veers and backtracks, its line of travel fits along the surface of a sphere.

Our observer might deduce from all this that the ship is being held to an invisible spherical surface by a force of gravity at the center of the sphere. Or he might decide that the ship is confined to a particular section of space and that section is curved in such a way as to force the ship to follow the course it does; a section of space is bent into a sphere. The choice, in other words, is between a force and a space geometry.

You may think this is an imaginary situation, but it isn't really. Our planet moves in an ellipse about the sun, as though it were sailing along some curved invisible surface. We explain the ellipse by supposing there is a force of gravity exerted between the sun and the earth that holds the earth in its orbit.

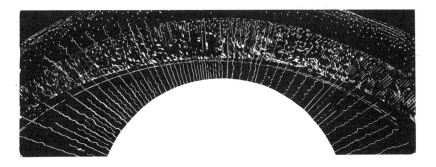

But suppose we consider space geometry instead. We could define the geometry of space not by looking at space itself, which is invisible and can't be seen, but by noting the manner in which objects move in it. If space were "flat," then objects would move through it in straight lines; if space were "curved," then objects would follow curved paths.

An object of a given mass and speed moving at a great distance from any other mass does indeed move in almost a straight line. If it approaches another mass, its path becomes more and more curved. Mass, apparently, curves space; the greater the mass and the closer, the sharper the curvature.

It may seem far more convenient and natural to talk of gravitation as a force rather than as space geometry — until light is considered. Light has no mass and should not be affected by gravitational force according to the older notions. If, however, light is traveling through curved space, then its path should curve too. Allowing for light's speed, the amount by which its path would be curved when passing near the sun's huge mass can be calculated.

In 1919, this part of Einstein's theory (announced three years before) was tested during an eclipse of the sun. The positions of stars near the sun were compared with their recorded positions when the sun was not in that part of the heavens. Einstein's theory was upheld and it seemed more accurate to talk about gravity in terms of curved space than in terms of force.

It is only fair to say, though, that in 1967 certain delicate measurements of the sun's shape brought Einstein's theory of gravitation into question. What will happen now and in the future we will have to wait and see.

43

In many science fiction stories I read about "force fields" and "hyperspace." What are these and do they really exist?

Every subatomic particle gives rise to one or more of four different kinds of influences. These are the gravitational, electromagnetic, weak nuclear, and strong nuclear. Each influence spreads out from its source of origin as a "field" that, in theory, pervades the entire universe. Similar fields from large numbers of particles can add their separate influences and produce terrifically intense resultant fields. Thus, the gravitational field is by far the weakest of the four, but the gravitational field of the sun, a body made up of a vast number of particles, is enormous.

Two particles within such a field may be made to move toward each other or away from each other, depending on the nature of the particles and of the field, and with an acceleration depending on how far apart they are. Such accelerations are usually interpreted as caused by "forces," so we speak of "force fields." In this sense, they really exist.

The force fields we know, however, always have matter as their source and don't exist in the absence of matter. In science fiction stories, on the other hand, it is often useful to imagine the construction of strong force fields without matter. One can then have a section of vacuum which will serve as a barrier to particles and radiation just as though it were a solid piece of steel six feet thick. It would have all the interatomic forces but none of the atoms that give rise to those forces. Such "matter-free force fields" are a convenient science fictional device but, alas, have no basis in the science we know today.

"Hyperspace" is another convenient science fictional device; one intended to get around the speed-of-light barrier.

To see how it works, think of a large, flat sheet of paper on which there are two dots six feet apart. Next, imagine an extremely slow snail that can only travel a foot an hour. Clearly, it will take him six hours to travel from one dot to another.

But suppose we bend the essentially two-dimensional sheet of paper through the third dimension, so as to bring the two dots close together. If they are now only a tenth of an inch apart and if the snail can somehow cross the air gap between the two ends of the piece of paper which have been curved toward each other in this fashion, he can go from one dot to the other in just half a minute.

Now for the analogy. If two stars are fifty light-years apart, then a spaceship going at maximum speed, that of light, will take fifty years to go from one to the other (relative to someone in either one of these star systems). This creates a great many complications and science fiction writers find they can simplify their plots if they pretend that the essentially three-dimensional structure of space can be folded through a fourth spatial dimension so that the stars are separated by only a small fourth-dimensional gap. The ship then crosses this gap and goes from one star to the other in a very short period of time.

It is customary for mathematicians to speak of objects with four dimensions by referring to analogous three-dimensional objects and adding the prefix "hyper," a Greek expression meaning "above," "over," or "beyond." An object whose surface is equally distant from the center in all four dimensions is a "hypersphere." Similarly, we can have a "hypertetrahedron," "hypercube," and a "hyperellipsoid." Using this convention, we can speak of the fourth-dimensional gap between the stars as "hyperspace."

But, alas, however convenient hyperspace may be to the science fiction writer, there is nothing in the science we know to show that it exists as anything but a mathematical abstraction.

44

What is antigravity? How can it be studied?

There are two types of fields, electromagnetic and gravitational, which fall off in intensity as the square of the distance. This fall in intensity is slow enough to enable an electromagnetic or gravitational field to be detectable at large distances. The earth is firmly held in the grip of the sun's gravitational field even though the sun is 93 million miles away.

The gravitational field is far the weaker of the two, however. The electromagnetic field set up by an electron is something like 4 million trillion trillion trillion times as strong as the gravitational field it sets up.

Of course, gravitational fields *seem* strong. We all have a painful experience concerning the strength of the earth's gravitational field every time we fall. But that is only because the earth is so huge. Every tiny fragment of it contributes to the gravitational field and in the end the total is enormous.

But suppose we take 100 million electrons (a quantity too little to see in a microscope if collected in one spot) and scatter them through a volume the size of the earth. They would set up an electromagnetic field equal to the gravitational field of the entire massive earth.

Why aren't we more aware of electromagnetic fields than of gravitational fields?

That is where another difference comes in. There are two kinds of electric charge, called positive and negative, so that an electromagnetic field can result in attraction (between a positive and a negative charge) or repulsion (between two positive or two negative charges). In fact, if the earth's volume contained nothing but 100 million electrons, those electrons would repel each other and scatter far and wide.

The forces of electromagnetic attraction and repulsion serve to mix positive and negative charges thoroughly, so that the effect of those charges tends to be canceled out. Very tiny electron excesses and deficiencies can be brought about and it is the electromagnetic fields of those tiny excesses and deficiencies that we study.

The gravitational field, however, seems to produce *only* a force of attraction. Every object possessing mass attracts every other object possessing mass, and as mass piles up so does the intensity of the gravitational field without any cancellation.

If a massive object *repelled* another massive object with the same intensity and in the same manner as those objects attract each other under the usual gravitational conditions, then we would have "antigravity" or "negative gravity."

Such gravitational repulsion has never been detected, but that may be because all the ordinary objects we can study in detail are made up of ordinary particles.

There are also "antiparticles," which are just like the common particles we know, except for the reversal of the electromagnetic field. Where a particular particle has a negative charge, the corresponding antiparticle has a positive charge, and so on. Perhaps antiparticles have the gravitational field reversed also. Two antiparticles would then attract each other gravitationally just as two particles do, but an antiparticle would *repel* an ordinary one.

The trouble is that a gravitational field is so weak it can't be detected in individual particles or antiparticles but only for sizable masses. We have sizable masses of particles but no one has ever collected a sizable mass of antiparticles in one place. Nor has anyone ever suggested any practical alternate way of detecting antigravitational effects.

45

What is the speed of gravitation?

A longer, but perhaps clearer, way of putting the question is this: Suppose the sun suddenly ceased to exist and vanished into nothingness. How long would it be before the earth would cease to be held by its gravitational field?

A similar question might be: How long after the sun disappears would the earth cease receiving its light?

We know the answer to the second question quite well. We know that the sun is just under 93 million miles from earth and we also know that light travels at 186,282 miles per second through a vacuum. The last bit of light leaving the sun, just before it disappeared, would take 8.3 minutes to reach the earth. In other words, we would see the sun disappear 8.3 minutes after it really disappeared.

The reason it is easy to answer the question about light is that there are a number of ways of actually measuring the speed at which light travels. These measurements are made practical by our ability to detect changes in the very faint light emitted by a distant heavenly body, and by our own ability to produce quite strong beams of light.

We don't have these advantages with gravitational fields. It is very difficult to study faint changes in weak gravitational fields and we can't produce strong gravitational effects extending over long distances here on earth.

So we have to fall back on theory. There are four types of interactions known in the universe: 1) strong nuclear, 2) weak nuclear, 3) electromagnetic, and 4) gravitational. Of these the first two are short-range, falling off very rapidly with distance. At distances greater than the width of an atomic nucleus, the nuclear interactions are so weak they can be ignored. The electromagnetic and gravitational in-

teractions are long-range, however. They fall off only as the square of the distance. This means they can make themselves felt even over astronomical distances.

Physicists believe that every interaction between two bodies takes place through the exchange of subatomic particles. The more massive the exchange particle, the shorter-range the interaction. Thus, the strong nuclear interaction results from the exchange of pions which are 270 times as massive as electrons. The weak nuclear interaction results from the exchange of even more massive W-particles (which haven't been detected yet, by the way).

If an exchange particle has no mass at all, then the interaction is as long-range as possible, and this is the case with the electromagnetic interaction. The exchange particle there is the massless photon. A stream of such massless photons makes up a beam of light or related radiations. The gravitational interaction, exactly as long-range as the electromagnetic one, must also involve a massless exchange particle — which is called a graviton.

But physicists have strong reason to suppose that massless particles can travel through a vacuum only at the speed of light; that is, at 186,282 miles per second, neither more nor less.

If this is so, then gravitons travel at exactly the speed of photons. This means that if the sun were to disappear, the last gravitons it emits would reach us at just the same time that the last photons would. At the instant we saw the sun disappear, we would also cease to be under its gravitational pull.

In other words, gravitation travels at the speed of light.

46

What is the unified field theory?

In the middle of the nineteenth century, four phenomena were known which could make their effects felt across a vacuum. These were: 1) gravitation, 2) light, 3) electrical attraction and repulsion, and 4) magnetic attraction and repulsion.

The four phenomena seemed at first to be completely independent, to have no necessary connection with one another. Between 1864 and 1873, however, the Scottish theoretical physicist J. Clerk Maxwell analyzed electrical and magnetic phenomena mathematically. He found he could work out certain basic relationships ("Maxwell's equations") which would describe both electrical and magnetic phenomena in such a way as to show that each was dependent upon the other. You couldn't have an electrical effect without a certain fixed magnetic effect as well — and vice versa. In other words, one could speak of an "electromagnetic field" that stretched out across a vacuum, which would affect bodies it touched according to the intensity of the field at that point in space.

Furthermore, Maxwell showed that if this field were made to oscillate in a regular fashion, it would give rise to a radiation that would move away from the source of oscillation at the speed of light in all directions. Light itself was such an "electromagnetic radiation," and Maxwell predicted the existence of forms of light with wavelengths much greater and much smaller than ordinary light. These other forms of light were discovered over the next couple of decades, and now one speaks of an entire "electromagnetic spectrum."

Thus, of the four phenomena mentioned at the beginning of this essay, three (electricity, magnetism, and light) were combined into a single field. But that still left gravity unaccounted for. We had 1) an electromagnetic field and 2) a gravitational field, and these still seemed to be two independent fields.

Physicists, however, felt it would be neater if there were only a single field (this is the "unified field theory"), and they have been searching for ways of describing both electromagnetic effects and gravitational effects in such a way that the existence of one could be made to describe the nature of the existence of the other.

Even if equations were discovered that would combine electromagnetic and gravitational effects, they would still fall short, by modern standards, of supplying us with a truly unified field. In the years since 1935, two new types of fields have been discovered, both affecting subatomic particles only and, even then, only at distances no greater than that of the diameter of the atomic nucleus. These are the "strong nuclear interaction" and the "weak nuclear interaction."

A true unified field would have to account for all four fields now known.

47

What is, briefly and simply, Einstein's theory of relativity?

According to the laws of motion first worked out in detail by Isaac Newton in the 1680s different motions add together according to the rules of simple arithmetic. Suppose a train is passing you at 20 miles an hour and a boy on the train throws a ball at 20 miles an hour in the direction of the train's motion. To the boy, moving with the train, the ball is moving 20 miles an hour. To you, however, the motion of the train and ball add together and the ball is moving at the rate of 40 miles an hour.

Thus, you see, one cannot speak of the ball's speed all by itself. What counts is its speed *relative to* a particular observer. Any theory of motion that attempts to explain the way velocities (and related phenomena) seem to vary from observer to observer would be a "theory of relativity."

Einstein's particular theory of relativity arose out of the fact that what works for thrown balls on trains doesn't seem to work for light. Light might be made to travel with the earth's motion, or against it. In the former case it should seem to travel more rapidly than in the latter (just as a plane moves more rapidly, relative to the ground, when it has a tailwind than when it is flying into the wind). However, the most careful measurements of light's velocity showed that it never varied, no matter what the nature of the motion of the source giving out the light.

Einstein therefore said: Let's suppose that when the velocity of light in a vacuum is measured, it always turns out to have the same value (about 186,282 miles per second) under all circumstances. How can we arrange the laws of the universe to account for that?

Einstein found that, in order to account for the constancy of light's velocity, one had to accept a great many unexpected phenomena.

He found that objects would have to grow shorter in the direction of their motion, shorter and shorter as their velocity increased until their length was zero at the velocity of light; that moving objects would have to increase in mass more and more as their velocity increased until that mass was infinite at the velocity of light; that the rate at which time progressed on a moving body decreased more and more as velocity increased until it stopped altogether at the velocity of light; that mass was equivalent to a certain amount of energy and vice versa.

All this he worked out in 1905, for bodies moving at constant velocity, as the "special theory of relativity." In 1915, he worked out even more subtle consequences for objects moving at varying velocity, including a new description of the behavior of gravitational effects. This is the "general theory of relativity."

The changes predicted by Einstein are noticeable only at great velocities. Such great velocities have been noted among subatomic particles and the changes predicted by Einstein have been checked and found to be present, very accurately present. Indeed, our atom-smashing devices couldn't work if Einstein's theory of relativity was incorrect; our atom bombs wouldn't explode; certain astronomical observations couldn't be made.

At ordinary speeds, however, the changes predicted by Einstein are so tiny they can be ignored. The simple arithmetic of Newton's laws works under these circumstances, and because we are always surrounded by the working of those laws, they come to seem like "common sense" to us, while Einstein's law seems "strange."

48

Why can't matter travel faster than the speed of light? (Part One)

Energy added to a body can affect it in a number of ways. If a hammer strikes a nail in midair, the nail goes flying off, gaining kinetic energy, or, in other words, energy of motion. If a hammer strikes a nail embedded in hard wood, so that the nail can't move, the nail still gains energy — but in the form of heat.

Albert Einstein, in his theory of relativity, showed that mass could be viewed as a form of energy (and the invention of the atom bomb certainly proved him correct). If energy is added to a body, that energy may therefore appear in the form of mass, as well as in other forms.

Under ordinary conditions, the gain of energy in the form of mass is so incomprehensibly tiny that no one could ever measure it. It was only in the twentieth century, when subatomic particles were observed to move at speeds of tens of thousands of miles per second, that examples of mass increase were found that were large enough to be detectable. A body moving at 160,000 miles a second relative to ourselves would be measured by us as having twice as much mass as when it was at rest relative to ourselves.

If energy is added to any freely moving body, that energy can enter the body in one of two ways: 1) as velocity, so that its speed of motion increases, and 2) as mass, so that it becomes "heavier." The division between these two forms of energy gain, as measured by ourselves, depends upon the speed of the body to begin with, again as measured by ourselves.

If the body is going at ordinary velocities, virtually all the added energy enters the body as velocity, and the body moves faster and faster with hardly any change in mass.

As the speed of the moving body increases (and as we imagine additional energy constantly being pumped into it), less and less of the energy enters as velocity and more and more as mass. We note that, though the body is still moving faster and faster, its rate of gaining speed is falling off. Instead, we note that it is becoming more massive at a slightly greater rate.

As its speed increases still further and gets fairly close to the 186,282 miles per second that is the speed of light in a vacuum, almost all the added energy enters as mass. In other words, the speed of motion of the body increases very slowly, but now it is the mass that is moving upward by leaps and bounds. By the time the speed of light is reached, *all* the added energy is appearing as additional mass.

The body *cannot* go faster than the speed of light because to make it do so one must impart additional energy to it and, at the speed of light, all that additional energy, however great, will merely be converted into additional mass, and the body will not increase its speed one iota.

Nor is this "just theory." Scientists have been carefully observing speeding subatomic particles for years. Cosmic ray particles exist with unimaginably high energy contents, yet though their mass climbs high indeed, their speeds never quite reach that of light in a vacuum. The mass and velocity of subatomic particles work out to just what the theory of relativity predicts and the speed of light is a maximum speed as a matter of observed fact and is *not* merely speculation.

49

Why can't matter travel faster than the speed of light? (Part Two)

The preceding explanation did not settle matters entirely. Instead it raised doubts and letters arrived asking further questions. Some have asked, "Why does the energy go into mass instead of velocity?" or "Why does light travel at 186,282 miles per second instead of at another speed?"

As of now, the only possible answer to such questions is "Because that's the way the universe is."

Others have asked, "In what way is mass increased?" That is easier. It is not by increasing the number of atoms. That stays the same. Each atom — indeed, each particle within the atom — increases in mass.

Some questioned whether we might not increase our resources by making matter move so fast that it would double its mass. Then we would have twice as much.

Not really. The increase in mass is not "real." It is a matter of measurement. Velocity only has meaning as a measurement relative to something else — to the person doing the measurement, for instance. It is only the measuring that counts. It is impossible for you to *measure* matter going faster than light.

But suppose you grabbed on to the matter, which you had measured as having twice its normal mass, in order to use it for some purpose. If you traveled with it, then its velocity relative to you is zero and suddenly its mass is normal.

If you flashed by a friend at nearly the speed of light you would measure his mass as very high and he would measure your mass as very high. Each of you would think his own mass was normal.

You might say, "But which has *really* increased in mass?" The answer is "It depends on who is doing the measuring." There's no such thing as "really"; everything is only as it is measured relative to something else by somebody. Hence the name, theory of "relativity."

You think you are standing heads up and that the Australians are standing heads down. But the Australians think they are heads up and you heads down. Which view is "really" correct? Neither. There's no such thing as "really." It depends on where you are standing on earth. All is relative.

Some have asked, "If mass goes up with velocity, then wouldn't it go down to zero if an object were standing absolutely still?" There is no such thing as "absolutely still," however. There is only "relative rest." Something can be at rest relative to something else. When an object is at rest relative to the person doing the measurement, it has a certain minimum mass called "rest mass." Mass can't be less than that.

A high relative velocity doesn't merely increase the measured mass of an object. It also decreases the measured length of the object in the direction it is traveling and slows up the measured passage of time on that object.

And if you ask why, the answer is "Because if that didn't happen, the speed of light would not be the maximum speed for matter."

50

Light is given off by particles traveling faster than light. How is this possible if nothing travels faster than light?

It is often stated that particles cannot travel "faster than light" and that the "speed of light" is the ultimate limit of speed.

Actually, if we say this we are not saying enough, for light travels at different speeds through different media. Light travels fastest through a vacuum, in which case it moves at a speed of 186,282 miles per second. It is *this* which is the ultimate speed.

We should say, then, that particles cannot travel "faster than the speed of light in a vacuum," if we want to be accurate.

Light traveling through any transparent medium other than a vacuum always travels more slowly than it does in a vacuum, in some cases much more slowly. The more slowly it travels in a particular medium, the greater the angle through which it bends (refraction) when it enters that medium from a vacuum at an oblique angle. The amount of bending is defined by a quantity termed the "index of refraction."

If the speed of light in a vacuum is divided by the index of refraction of a particular medium, we find the speed of light in that medium. The index of refraction of air at ordinary pressures and temperatures is about 1.0003, so that the speed of light in air is 186,282 divided by 1.0003, or 186,225 miles per second. This is 56 miles per second less than the speed of light in a vacuum.

The index of refraction of water is 1.33, of ordinary kinds of glass 1.7, and of diamond 2.42. This means that light travels at a speed of 140,000 miles per second through water, 110,000 miles per second through glass, and only 77,000 miles per second through diamond.

Particles can't travel faster than 186,282 miles per second, but they can surely travel at, say, 160,000 miles per second, even through water.

When they do this they are traveling through water faster than the speed of light *in water.* In fact, it is possible for particles to travel faster than light in any medium *but* a vacuum.

Particles traveling faster than light in some nonvacuum medium emit a blue light that trails behind. The angle at which it trails behind depends on how much faster than the speed of light in that medium the particle is going.

The first to observe this blue light emitted by faster-than-light particles was a Russian physicist named Pavel A. Cerenkov, who reported it in 1934. The light is therefore called "Cerenkov radiation." In 1937, two other Russian physicists, Ilya M. Frank and Igor Y. Tamm, explained the existence of this light by relating it to the relative speeds of particle and light in that medium. The result was that in 1958 all three men were awarded the Nobel Prize in physics.

Special instruments, "Cerenkov counters," have been designed to detect such radiation and measure its intensity and the direction in which it is given off.

Cerenkov counters are particularly useful because they are activated only by very fast particles and because the speed of those particles is easily estimated from the angle at which the light is emitted. Very energetic cosmic rays move at a speed so close to that of light in a vacuum that they will produce Cerenkov radiation even in air.

Tachyons, which are hypothetical particles that can only move *faster* than the speed of light in a vacuum, would leave a very brief flash of Cerenkov radiation even in a vacuum. It is by detecting such Cerenkov radiation that physicists hope to prove the actual existence of tachyons (*if* they exist).

51

If nothing is faster than light, what are tachyons, which are supposed to move faster than light?

Einstein's special theory of relativity requires that any object that exists in our universe cannot be made to go at a measured velocity greater than that of light in a vacuum. It would take an infinite amount of energy to force it merely to light velocity and the more-than-infinite amount required to shove it beyond that point is unthinkable.

But just suppose an object *were* moving faster than light.

Light travels at 186,282 miles per second, but what if a certain one-pound, one-inch-long object happened to be traveling at 263,000 miles per second. If we use Einstein's equations, it turns out that the object would then be $-\sqrt{-1}$ pounds in mass and $+\sqrt{-1}$ inches long.

In other words, any object moving faster than light would have to have a mass and a length expressed in what mathematicians call "imaginary numbers" (see question 6). We have no way of visualizing masses or lengths that are expressed in imaginary numbers, so it is easy to assume that such things, being unthinkable, don't exist.

In 1967, however, Gerald Feinberg of Columbia University wondered if it were fair to do that. (Feinberg was not the first to suggest the particle; that credit belongs to O. M. Bilaniuk and E. C. G. Sudarshan. Feinberg popularized the notion, however.) Perhaps an "imaginary" mass and length is merely a way of describing an object with (let us say) negative gravity — an object that repels matter in our universe instead of being gravitationally attracted.

Feinberg called these faster-than-light, imaginary-mass-and-length particles "tachyons," from a Greek word meaning "swift." If we grant the existence of these tachyons, can they otherwise follow the requirements of Einstein's equations?

Apparently they can. We can picture a whole universe of tachyons going faster than the speed of light yet following the requirements of relativity. In order for them to do so though, the situation, as far as energy and velocity are concerned, is the reverse of what we are accustomed to.

In our "slow universe," a motionless body has zero energy, but as it gains energy it moves faster and faster, and at infinite energy it speeds up to light velocity. In the "swift universe," a tachyon with zero energy moves at infinite speed; and the more energy it gains the *slower* it moves, until with infinite energy it *slows down* to light velocity.

In our slow universe, a body cannot go faster than light under any circumstances. In the swift universe, a tachyon cannot go slower than light under any circumstances. The light velocity is the boundary between the two universes and it cannot be crossed.

But do tachyons really exist? We might decide that it is possible to have a swift universe that does not violate Einstein's theory; but to be possible doesn't necessarily mean to *be*.

One possible way of detecting the swift universe is to consider that if a tachyon moves through a vacuum at faster-than-light speeds, it must leave a trail of potentially detectable light as it goes. Of course, most tachyons would go extremely fast — millions of times as fast as light (just as most ordinary objects move quite slowly, only a millionth the speed of light).

Ordinary tachyons and their flashes of light would have passed us long before we could spot them. Only the very occasional high-energy tachyons would pass us at speeds nearly as slow as that of light. Even then, these would cover a mile in something like 1/200,000 of a second, and spotting them would be a most delicate operation.

52

Tachyons with zero energy move at infinite speed. Is infinite speed really possible?

The thought of a particle moving at infinite speed has its paradoxes. It would go from A to B in zero time, which means it would be at both A and B at the same time, as well as in all places in between. It would continue going on to points C, D, E, and so on through an infinite distance, all in zero time. A particle moving at infinite speed would therefore have the properties of a solid rod of infinite length.

If space curves, as Einstein's theory of relativity suggests, the solid rod would actually be a vast circle, or spiral, or a bumpy curve of even more complicated form.

But let us assume there is a universe of tachyons, particles which all possess speeds greater than light. As such particles gain more and more energy, they go more and more slowly, till at infinite energies they slow down to the speed of light. As they lose more and more energy, they go more and more quickly, till at zero energy they go at infinite speed.

We can imagine that in such a universe, there would be particles with a wide range of energies; some very energetic, some very unenergetic, and some in between. (As is true of particles in our universe.)

The passage of energy from one particle to another in such a universe (as in our own) would have to be through some interaction; as for instance, through a collision. If low-energy particle A collided with high-energy particle B, the chances are very great that A would gain energy at the expense of B, so there would be a general tendency toward the formation of intermediate-energy particles.

Of course, there would be exceptions. If two particles of equal energy interact, one may gain energy at the expense of the other, broadening the range. It is even possible (though unlikely) that a high-energy particle may gain still more energy by colliding with a low-energy particle, leaving the low-energy particle with less energy than before.

A consideration of the random nature of such collisions and the random nature of energy transfer leads to the conclusion that there will be a range of energies, with most of the particles being of intermediate-energy; some being high- (or low-) energy; a few being very high- (or very low-) energy; a tiny quantity being very, very high- (or very, very low-) energy; and just a trace being very, very, very high- (or very, very, very, low-) energy.

This distribution of energies over a range can be expressed mathematically and it would be seen that no particle would actually have either infinite energy or zero energy; these values would be closely approached but never reached. Tachyons would sometimes move at very slightly more than the speed of light but never at exactly the speed of light; and tachyons might go at truly enormous speeds, a million (or a billion or a trillion) times the speed of light, but never at truly infinite speeds.

Suppose two tachyons of exactly the same energies hit each other exactly dead center head on. Might not the kinetic energies of both exactly cancel and the two then leave the site of collision at truly infinite velocities? Again this is an idea which can be approached but not reached. The chance of both tachyons having *exactly* equal energies and meeting *exactly* head on are vanishingly small.

In other words, truly infinite speed would be approached but not reached in the universe of tachyons — and we don't have to worry, in this case, about the paradoxes to which the infinite always seems to give rise.

53

What is the Heisenberg uncertainty principle?

To explain the matter of uncertainty, let's begin by asking what certainty is? When you know something for sure, and exactly, about some object, you are certain about that piece of data, whatever it is.

And how do you get to know that something? One way or another, you must interact with the object. You must weigh it to see how heavy it is, pound it to see how hard it is, or perhaps just look at it to see where it is. But there must be interaction, however gentle.

It can be argued that this interaction always introduces some change into the very property you are trying to determine. In other words, learning something changes that something through the very act of learning about it, so that you haven't quite learned it exactly, after all.

For instance, suppose you want to measure the temperature of hot bath water? You put in a thermometer and measure the water's temperature. But the thermometer is cold and its presence in the water cools the water just a bit. You can still get a good approximation of the temperature, but not *exactly* to the trillionth of a degree. The thermometer has almost immeasurably changed the temperature it was measuring.

Again, suppose you want to measure the air pressure in a tire. You use a little plunger that is pushed out by a tiny bit of escaping air. But the fact that air escapes means that the air pressure has been lowered just a tiny bit by the act of measuring it.

Is it possible to invent measuring devices so tiny and sensitive and indirect as not to introduce any change at all in the property being measured?

A German physicist, Werner Heisenberg, decided in 1927 that it was not. A measuring device can only be so tiny. It could be as small as a subatomic particle, but no smaller. It had to make use of as little as one quantum of energy, but no less. A single particle and a single quantum of energy are enough to introduce certain changes. If you simply look at something in order to see it, you do so by virtue of light photons bouncing off the object, and that introduces a change.

Such changes are extremely tiny and we can and do ignore them in ordinary life — but the changes are still there. And what if you are dealing with extremely tiny objects where even extremely tiny changes loom large.

If you wanted to tell the position of an electron, for instance, you'd have to bounce a light quantum off it, or more likely a gamma ray photon, in order to "see" it. And that bouncing photon would knock the electron away.

Heisenberg succeeded in demonstrating, in particular, that it is impossible to devise any method for *exactly* determining both the position and momentum of any object simultaneously. The more closely you determine the position, the less closely you can determine the momentum, and vice versa. He worked out just how large the inexactness or "uncertainty" of these properties would have to be, and this is his "uncertainty principle."

The principle implies a certain "graininess" to the universe. If you try to enlarge a newspaper picture, you eventually get to the point where you see the little grains or dots and you lose all detail. The same is true if you look too closely at the universe.

Some people are disappointed at this and feel it to be a confession of eternal ignorance. Not at all. We are interested in learning how the universe works, and the principle of uncertainty is a key factor in that working. The "graininess" is there, that's all. Heisenberg has showed it to us, and physicists are grateful.

54

What is parity?

Suppose we give each subatomic particle one of two labels, A or B. Suppose, further, that whenever an A particle broke up to form two particles, those two particles would be either both A or both B. We could then write A = A + A or A = B + B. If a B particle broke up to form the two particles, then one of those particles would always be A and the other B, so that we could write B = A + B.

You might discover other situations, too. If two particles collided and broke up to form three particles you might find that A + A = A + B + B, or that A + B = B + B + B.

Some situations would not be observed, however. You would *not* find, for instance, that A + B = A + A, or that A + B + A = B + A + B.

What does this all mean? Well, suppose you think of A as any even integer such as 2, 4, or 6, and B as any odd integer such as 3, 5, or 7. Two even integers always add up to an even integer (6 = 2 + 4) so A = A + A. Two odd integers always add up to an even integer, too (8 = 3 + 5) so A = B + B. The sum of an odd and an even integer, however, is always an odd integer (7 = 3 + 4) so B = A + B.

In other words, certain subatomic particles could be called "odd" and certain others could be called "even," for they form only those combinations and breakdowns which hold true in the case of adding odd and even integers.

When two integers are both even or both odd, mathematicians say they are of "the same parity"; if one is even and one is odd they are of "different parity." Therefore when subatomic particles act as though some are odd and some are even and the rules of adding odd and even are never broken, that is considered "conservation of parity."

In 1927, the physicist Eugene Wigner showed that there was conservation of parity among subatomic particles, because those particles could be considered as having "right-left symmetry." Objects possessing such symmetry are identical with their mirror images. The numerals 8 and 0 and the letters H and X have such symmetry. If you flipped 8, 0, H, or X so that right became left and vice versa, you would still have 8, 0, H, and X. The letters b and p do not have such right-left symmetry. If you flip them, then b becomes d and p becomes q — different letters altogether.

In 1956, two physicists, Tsung Dao Lee and Chen Ning Yang, showed that parity ought not be conserved for certain types of subatomic events, and experiments quickly showed they were right. This meant that certain subatomic particles acted as though they were not symmetrical under certain conditions.

For this reason, a more general conservation law was worked out. Where a particular particle was not symmetrical, then its antiparticle (with an opposite electric charge or magnetic field) was also not symmetrical, but in the opposite fashion. Thus, if a particle resembled p, then its antiparticle resembled q.

If the electric charge (C) and the parity (P) are taken together, then a simple rule could be set up describing which subatomic events could take place and which could not. This is called "CP-conservation."

Later, it was decided that in order to make the rule really foolproof, one ought also to consider the direction of time (T); for a subatomic event can be viewed as happening either forward in time or backward in time. This is called "CPT-conservation."

Recently, even CPT-conservation came into question, but no final decision has yet been reached there.

55

Why do we talk about the half-life of an isotope? Why not the whole life?

Some atoms are unstable. Such an atom, left to itself, will sooner or later spontaneously undergo a change. An energetic particle or a gamma ray photon will come flying out of its nucleus and it will become a different kind of atom. (A particular kind of atom can be called an isotope.) A quantity of unstable atoms in one place will radiate particles or gamma rays in all directions, so such atoms are said to be radioactive.

There is no way of telling when a particular radioactive atom is going to undergo a change. It may do so within a second. It may not do so for a year. It may not do so for a trillion years. Therefore, you cannot measure the "whole life" of a radioactive atom, the time during which it will remain unchanged. This "whole life" can have any value, so there's no use talking about it.

Suppose, though, that you have a great many atoms of a particular radiactive isotope in one place. At any given moment, some of them are undergoing change. You will find that although you can't, under any circumstances, tell when a particular atom will change, you *can* predict that so many atoms out of, let us say, a trillion trillion, will change after so many seconds.

It is a matter of statistics. There is no way in which you can tell whether a particular American will be killed in an auto accident in a particular year or not, but it *is* possible to predict with considerable accuracy that a certain number of Americans will die in auto accidents in a particular year.

Given a large number of atoms of a particular isotope, one can measure the quantity of radiation at a given time and be able to predict how much radiation (how many changing atoms) there will be at any future time. It turns out that, given the way in which the changes take place, it always takes the same time for 1/10 of all the atoms to change, regardless of how many you start with. In fact, it always takes some fixed time for 2/10 of them to change, or 4/17, or 19/573, or *any* particular fraction, no matter how many atoms you start with.

So instead of talking about the "whole life" of the atoms of a particular isotope — which is worthless — you talk about the length of time it takes some fraction of them to change, for this length of time is easily measured. But why just *some* fraction? The simplest of all fractions is ½, so it is common to speak of the time it takes for half the atoms of a particular isotope to undergo change, and that is the "half-life" of that isotope.

The more stable a particular isotope is, the less likely its atoms are to undergo change and the less likely it is that a particular number of atoms are going to change within an hour, say, after you start your observations. That means it will take longer for half the atoms to change.

In other words, the longer the half-life of a particular isotope, the more stable it is; the shorter the half-life, the less stable.

Some half-lives can be very long indeed. The isotope thorium-232 has a half-life of 14 billion years. It would take that long for half of any quantity of thorium-232 to break down. That is why there is still plenty of thorium-232 in the earth's crust, even though it has been there (and steadily breaking down) for nearly 5 billion years.

Some half-lives can be very short indeed. The half-life of the isotope helium-5 is about a billionth of a trillionth of a second.

56

Why are scientists finding so many new subatomic particles, and what is their significance?

The key to the answer of this question lies in one phrase: "More energy."

Physicists study the inner structure of the atomic nucleus in a very crude way. They hit it with all their might with subatomic particles, smash the nucleus into fragments, and then study the pieces.

What has changed over the last thirty years has been the energy with which the tiny subatomic "bullets" are sent smashing into the atomic nucleus. In the 1930s, those bullets had energies in the millions of electron volts; in the 1940s, in the hundreds of millions; in the 1950s, in the billions; and in the 1960s, in the dozens of billions. It seems that in the 1970s we will probably have bullets that number in the hundreds of billions of electron volts.

The more energetically the nucleus is smashed into, the greater the number of particles that emerge and the more unstable they are. You might suppose that as the smashes grow harder, the emerging particles will be smaller. (After all, a hard smash will split a rock into two large pieces, but a harder smash will split that same rock into a dozen small pieces.) This is not so in the case of nuclei. The particles that emerge tend to be quite heavy.

Energy, you see, can be converted into mass. The subatomic particles that appear in an atom-smashing process are not knocked out of the nucleus as though they were there all along. They are formed at the moment of smash out of the energy of the smashing particles. The greater the energy of the incoming particle, the more massive the particle that can be formed, and usually the more unstable the particle.

In a sense, subatomic particles go flying out of smashed nuclei the way sparks fly off steel struck by flint. The sparks weren't in the steel to begin with; they were formed out of the energy of collision.

But in that case, is there any significance to all these new subatomic particles? Might they not just be the random products of energy, as sparks are?

Physicists don't think so, because there's too much order among them. The particles that are formed have certain properties that obey certain rather intricate rules. That is, the various particles can be represented by numbers that are identified by names such as "isotopic spin," "strangeness," "parity," and so on, and the nature of the numbers is dictated according to certain rigid limitations.

There must be something behind these limitations.

The American physicist Murray Gell-Mann has worked out a system of arranging the various subatomic particles according to these various numbers in regular progression, and in doing so he has been able to predict new and hitherto-unknown particles. In particular, he predicted the existence of an omega-minus particle with certain unlikely properties — but when it was looked for it was found, and with just those properties.

Gell-Mann also suggests that the hundreds of particles now known would naturally be arranged in the fashion he has shown if they were all built out of a very few kinds of still simpler particles he calls "quarks." Physicists are hunting for quarks now. If they are found, they may offer us a completely new view of the fundamental nature of matter and, just possibly, a vastly useful one.

57

What is a quark?

The notion of a quark originated from the fact that well over a hundred different kinds of subatomic particles have been discovered in the last quarter-century. To be sure, very few of them last for more than a billionth of a second before breaking down, but the mere fact of their existence puzzles physicists.

Why so many, each one different from the rest?

Can it be that the different particles can be grouped into several large families? Within each family, numerous particles might differ among themselves in very regular fashion. In that case, it would only be necessary to account for the existence of a few families of particles, rather than for every single particle separately. Some order would have been established out of what seemed a subatomic "jungle."

In 1961, the American physicist Murray Gell-Mann and the Israeli physicist Yuval Ne'emen independently worked out a system for organizing particles into such families. Gell-Mann even presented one family that included what he called an omega-minus particle with very odd and unusual properties, but one that had never been encountered. Knowing what properties it was supposed to have, physicists knew exactly what to look for. And in 1964 they found it, and discovered it to be exactly as Gell-Mann had described it.

Gell-Mann, studying his families, wondered if perhaps all the different subatomic particles could be built up of combinations of just a few still simpler particles. That would greatly simplify the view of the universe if it were so. It seemed to him that if one postulated three different subsubatomic particles of particular properties, one could arrange them in different ways and arrive at all the different subatomic particles known.

114

Because it took a combination of three such hypothetical particles to make up the known particles, Gell-Mann thought of a passage in James Joyce's *Finnegans Wake* (a book in which the author twisted and distorted words for literary purposes), which went "Three quarks for Musther Mark."

Gell-Mann called the hypothetical particles "quarks," therefore.

The amazing thing about the quarks is that they would have to have fractional electric charges. All known charges are equal to that on an electron (-1) or a proton ($+1$) or are exact multiples of those charges. The charge on the p-quark, however, was only $+\frac{2}{3}$ and on the n-quark and the lambda-quark $-\frac{1}{3}$ each. A proton, for instance, would be made up of one n-quark and two p-quarks, a neutron of two n-quarks and one p-quark, and so on.

But does the quark really exist? Or is it just a mathematical fiction?

To see what I mean, consider a dollar bill. A dollar bill can be considered as equal to ten dimes, but is that just a mathematical equation, or is it possible that you might tear up a dollar bill into ten pieces and find that each piece is a solid, metallic dime?

Ever since Gell-Mann first proposed the existence of quarks, physicists have been trying to locate some sign of them, but without success. In 1969, reports from Australia indicated that tracks of particles with fractional electric charge were located among the particle showers produced by cosmic ray collisions. The evidence, however, was very marginal and most physicists remained skeptical of the report.

58

It has been said that protons are built up of combinations of three quarks, and also that one quark is thirty times as massive as a proton. How can both statements be true?

Both statements can be true. At least, the two statements are not necessarily self-contradictory. The key to the resolution of the apparent contradiction is the fact that mass is an aspect of energy.

Every object can be considered as possessing kinetic energy relative to some appropriate frame of reference. The kinetic energy is equal to half the product of the object's mass and the square of its velocity. As its energy is increased, both the mass and the velocity increase (the velocity, mainly, at low energies, and the mass, mainly, at very high energies).

Consider next that the smaller objects are, and the more intimately joined, the stronger (in general) are the forces holding them together. Bodies of really large size, such as the sun and the earth, are held together by a gravitational field, which is the weakest, by far, of all known forces.

Atoms and molecules are held together by the much stronger electromagnetic field. Through that field, molecules are often held together quite firmly; the atoms within a molecule even more firmly; and the electrons and nuclei within an atom still more firmly.

The particles within an atomic nucleus are held together by a nuclear field, which is over a hundred times as strong as the electromagnetic field and which is, in fact, the strongest force known. (That is one reason why nuclear explosions are so much more violent than ordinary chemical explosions.)

If the protons (and neutrons) which are to be found within the nucleus are themselves made up of a number of still more fundamental particles, quarks, then the bonds holding the quarks together are very likely to be considerably stronger than those holding protons and neutrons together. A new field, much stronger than any now known, could well be involved.

In order to break up the individual proton or neutron into the quarks making it up, enormous energies must be poured into the proton or neutron — much greater energies than are required to chip away, successfully, at the conglomeration of protons and neutrons that make up the atomic nucleus.

When the proton or neutron breaks up, the quarks that appear pick up the energy that has been poured in. Some of that energy would make itself apparent as a large velocity, some as a large mass. In other words, thanks to the inpouring of enormous energies, the quark which, inside the proton, was only one third as massive as the proton, becomes, once it is isolated, many times as massive as the proton.

Once isolated, quarks would have an enormous tendency to rejoin because of the unprecedented intensity of the field through which they experience a mutual attraction. The rejoining would liberate enormous energies, and the loss of that energy would result in a loss of mass. The quarks would then shrink in mass sufficiently to have a combination of three be no more massive than a single proton.

So far, physicists simply don't have at their disposal the kinds of energies required to split subatomic particles into quarks, so they cannot easily test whether the quark hypothesis has real merit or not. Some cosmic ray particles do, however, have the energies, and the particle showers they produce on collision with atoms are being closely watched for quarks.

59

In the atom bomb, matter is converted into energy. Is it possible to do the reverse and convert energy into matter?

It is certainly possible to change energy into matter, but to do so in large quantities is impractical. Let us see why.

According to Einstein's special theory of relativity, $e = mc^2$, where e represents energy, measured in ergs, m represents mass in grams, and c is the speed of light in centimeters per second.

Light travels through a vacuum with a speed of very nearly 30 billion (3×10^{10}) centimeters per second. The quantity c^2 represents the product of $c \times c$; that is, $3 \times 10^{10} \times 3 \times 10^{10}$, or 9×10^{20}. This means that c^2 is equal to 900,000,000,000,000,000,000.

A mass of 1 gram ($m = 1$) can therefore be converted, in theory, into 9×10^{20} ergs of energy. The average American is more familiar with the ounce (equal to 28.35 grams) as a unit of mass. One ounce of matter represents 2.55×10^{22} ergs of energy.

The erg is a very small unit of energy. The more familiar kilocalorie is equal to nearly 42 billion ergs. An ounce of matter turned into energy would yield 6.1×10^{11} (or 610 billion) kilocalories. You can keep alive very comfortably on 2500 kilocalories a day, obtained from the food you eat. If you had the energy available to you that is represented by a single ounce of matter, you would have a supply that would last you 670,000 years, which is a lot by anybody's standards.

To put it another way, if the energy represented by a single ounce of matter could be turned completely into electrical energy, it would keep a hundred-watt electric light bulb burning continuously for 800,000 years.

To put it still another way, the energy represented by a single ounce of matter is equivalent to that obtained by burning 200 million gallons of gasoline.

118

It is no wonder, then, that in nuclear bombs, where sizable quantities of matter are turned into energy, so much destruction is turned loose in the explosion of one bomb.

The change works both ways. If matter can be turned into energy, then energy can be turned into matter. This can be done any time in the laboratory. A very energetic particle of energy — a gamma ray photon — can be converted into an electron and a positron without much trouble. The process is thereby reversed, and energy is, in this way, turned into matter.

The matter formed, however, consists of two very light particles, almost vanishingly small in mass. Can the same principle be used to form more matter — even enough matter to be seen?

Ah, but you can't beat the arithmetic. If an ounce of matter can be converted into as much energy as is produced by burning 200 million gallons of gasoline, then it will take all the energy produced by burning 200 million gallons of gasoline to manufacture a mere ounce of matter.

Even if someone were willing to make the demonstration and go to all the expense involved in collecting all that energy (and perhaps several times as much, allowing for inevitable wastage) just to form an ounce of matter, it still couldn't be done. All that energy simply could not be produced quickly enough and concentrated into a small enough volume to produce an ounce of matter all at once.

Thus, the conversion is possible in theory, but is completely impractical in practice. To be sure, the matter of the universe was once formed presumably from energy, but certainly not under any set of conditions we can possibly duplicate in the laboratory today.

119

60

Do antiparticles produce antienergy?

At the beginning of the twentieth century, physicists began to understand that all matter consisted of certain different kinds of particles. In 1930, an English physicist, Paul Dirac, working on the mathematical theory of those particles, decided that each type of particle ought to have its opposite.

For instance, the electron has a negative electric charge and the proton has a positive electric charge of exactly the same size, but the two particles are not opposites. The proton, it seems, is much more massive than the electron.

There ought to be, according to Dirac, a particle with the same mass as the electron but with a positive electric charge; and one with the same mass as the proton, but with a negative electric charge. These were indeed detected eventually, so that we now know of an "antielectron" (or "positron") and an "antiproton."

The neutron has no electric charge at all, but it has a magnetic field pointed in a certain direction. There is an "antineutron" which also has no electric charge but which has a magnetic field pointed in the opposite direction.

It seems to be a law of nature that one particle can be turned into another particle, but that whenever a particle is formed without the previous existence of a particle, an antiparticle must be formed with it.

Here is an example. A neutron will turn into a proton, and that in itself seems to be okay since one particle has turned into another. In the conversion, though, an electron is also formed. This means one particle has turned into two particles. To balance that second particle, a tiny antiparticle called an "antineutrino" is also formed.

120

A particle (the neutron) has turned into another particle (the proton) plus a particle/antiparticle pair (the electron and antineutrino).

Particle/antiparticle pairs can be formed out of energy, and particle/antiparticle pairs can be turned back into energy in any numbers. You can't form just a particle out of energy, or just an antiparticle — but you can form the pair.

Energy itself is made up of "photons" and a question arises as to whether a photon is a particle or an antiparticle. There seems no way of turning a photon into an electron, for instance, so it can't be a particle. There's no way of turning it into an antielectron, either, so it can't be an antiparticle.

However, a sufficiently energetic gamma ray photon can be turned into an electron/antielectron pair. It would seem, then, that the photon is itself neither a particle nor an antiparticle but a particle/antiparticle pair all by itself.

Every photon is an antiphoton as well. To put it another way, a photon is its own opposite.

You could look at it this way. Suppose you folded a sheet of paper down the middle, dividing it in two and put the names of all the particles on one side and the names of all the antiparticles on the other side. Where would you put the photon? Right on the crease!

For that reason the energy produced by a world of particles consists of photons and the energy produced by a world of antiparticles consists also of photons, with no difference between the two. The energy is the same either way and there is no such thing (as far as we know at present) as antienergy.

121

61

How do the properties of cosmic rays and neutrinos differ?

Cosmic rays consist of speeding subatomic particles of considerable mass, which carry positive electric charges. About 90 percent of the particles are protons (hydrogen nuclei) and 9 percent are alpha particles (helium nuclei). The remaining 1 percent are nuclei of more complex atoms. Nuclei of atoms as complex as iron, with 56 times the mass of a single proton, have been detected.

Because cosmic ray particles are so massive and move with such enormous velocities (nearly the speed of light), they carry a great deal of energy. They are the most energetic particles we know of, in fact, and some cosmic ray particles are billions of times as energetic as anything that can be produced in the very largest accelerators.

Cosmic ray particles smash into the earth's atmosphere, breaking up any atoms they encounter and producing floods of "secondary radiation" consisting of a variety of particles, including mesons and positrons. Eventually, the radiation smashes into the earth itself, some of it penetrating many yards into the ground before being absorbed. Such particles can bring about changes in any atoms they encounter, including those in the human body. The changes so brought about might, conceivably, produce diseases such as leukemia. They might also induce mutations. For any given individual, however, the chances of this happening are small, for almost all cosmic ray particles that happen to strike a particular person pass through him without significant harm.

The exact source of cosmic ray particles and the manner in which they gain their enormous energies are matters of dispute.

Neutrinos are produced, along with electrons, positrons, or muons, in any nuclear reaction that produces any of the latter. The nuclear reactions that go on in the sun, for instance, produce large quantities of positrons and therefore produce large quantities of neutrinos as well.

Neutrinos, which travel at the speed of light, are even faster than cosmic ray particles, but are much less energetic, for neutrinos are completely without mass and electric charge. Neutrinos are not absorbed by matter unless they make a direct hit upon an atomic nucleus, and this happens so rarely that they can, on the average, pass through trillions of miles of solid lead without being absorbed.

Thus, the countless trillions of neutrinos produced by the sun every second streak out in all directions. Those that happen to be aimed at the earth strike us, then pass right through the planet as though it were not there. They pass through all of us as well. We are bombarded by neutrinos constantly day and night all our lives. Since they pass through us without being absorbed, however, they do not affect us in any way.

It is possible, of course, that a particular neutrino may, through a very lucky chance, make a direct hit on an atomic nucleus just when it happens to be in our vicinity. It can then be detected. In the 1950s, physicists learned how to take advantage of these rare instances. Neutrinos may now serve to give us information about the interior of the stars (where they are formed) which we could not have learned in any other way.

62

How dangerous are cosmic rays to men in space?

Back in 1911, an Austrian physicist, Victor F. Hess, discovered that the earth was being bombarded with very penetrating radiation from outer space. This radiation was named "cosmic rays" in 1925 by the American physicist Robert A. Millikan because they originated in the "cosmos," or universe.

Over the years, it was discovered that cosmic rays consisted of very high-speed atomic nuclei, each carrying a positive electric charge. About 90 percent of them were protons (nuclei of hydrogen atoms) and 9 percent were alpha particles (nuclei of helium atoms). The remaining 1 percent are more massive and complicated nuclei, some as large as those of iron, fifty-six times as massive as the proton.

The speeding nuclei which strike the earth's outer atmosphere are the "primary radiation." They collide with air molecules and blow them apart, producing a variety of particles nearly as energetic as the primary radiation. These new particles, blasted out of air molecules, make up the "secondary radiation."

Some of the radiation reaches the surface of the earth and penetrates many feet into its crust. A bit of it passes through human bodies on the way. Such radiation may do occasional damage to cells, and this may be one of the factors that produces mutations in the genes. Enough of such radiation could damage enough cells to kill a person, but there just isn't that much of it here at the bottom of our atmosphere. Living creatures have survived cosmic ray bombardment for billions of years.

The origin of cosmic rays is a matter of dispute, but at least some of them are formed by ordinary stars. In 1942, it was discovered that our own sun produces mild cosmic rays when a "solar flare" (a kind of huge explosion) rocks its surface.

124

Our upper atmosphere absorbs much of the punch of the average cosmic ray particles, and the secondary radiation is absorbed, in part, farther down. Only a small fraction of the original energy of radiation survives to reach us here at the surface.

Out in space, however, astronauts would have to face the full fury of the primary radiation. Nor would shielding do much good. The cosmic ray particles striking the atoms in any shield would set off secondary radiation that would spray inward in all directions like shrapnel. The wrong kind of shielding might actually make matters worse.

The amount of the danger depends on just how much cosmic ray activity there is in outer space — especially on the number of the really massive particles, which would do the most damage. Numerous satellites have been sent into outer space by the United States and the Soviet Union to check on cosmic ray quantities, and it would seem that under ordinary conditions the amount is low enough for reasonable safety.

The greatest chance of danger may arise from the sun's mild cosmic rays. Our atmosphere stops those nearly completely, but there is no atmosphere to do that service for the astronauts. Although mild, their quantity may make them dangerous. The sun's cosmic rays are present in quantity only at times of solar flares. Fortunately, these flares don't occur very frequently, but unfortunately the exact time of their coming cannot be predicted.

While our astronauts are on the moon, therefore, we must just hope that for a week or two there are no major flares spewing out cosmic ray particles in their direction.

63

Are neutrinos matter or energy?

In the nineteenth century, scientists assumed that matter and energy were two entirely different things. Matter was anything which took up space and which possessed mass. Because it had mass, matter also had inertia and responded to a gravitational field. As for energy, that did not take up room and did not have mass, but it could do work. It was further felt that matter consisted of particles (atoms), whereas energy often consisted of waves.

Furthermore, nineteenth-century scientists felt that matter could neither be created nor destroyed, and that energy could neither be created nor destroyed. The total quantity of matter in the universe was constant and so was the total quantity of energy. Thus, there was a law of conservation of matter, and a law of conservation of energy as well.

Then in 1905, Albert Einstein demonstrated that mass is a very concentrated form of energy. Mass could be converted to energy and vice versa. All one had to take into account was the law of conservation of energy. That included matter.

What's more, by the 1920s it became clear that one couldn't speak of particles and waves as though they were two different things. What we ordinarily consider particles act like waves in some ways. What we ordinarily consider waves act like particles in some ways. Thus, we can speak of "electron waves," for instance; and we can also speak of "light particles," or "photons."

There still remains a difference. Particles of matter can be at rest relative to some observer. Even though they are at rest, they possess mass. They have a "rest mass" of more than zero.

Particles such as photons, however, have a rest mass of zero. If they were at rest relative to you, you could measure no mass at all. This is purely theoretical, though, for particles with a rest mass of zero can never be at rest with respect to you or to any observer. Such particles must always travel at a speed of 186,282 miles per second through a vacuum. As soon as they are formed, they dash off at that speed.

It is because photons always travel at 186,282 miles per second (through a vacuum) and because light is made up of photons that we speak of this velocity as the "speed of light."

Well, what about neutrinos? They are formed in certain nuclear reactions and no atomic physicist has yet been able to measure their mass. It seems quite likely that neutrinos, like photons, have a rest mass of zero.

If so, neutrinos always travel at 186,282 miles per second through a vacuum and assume that speed the instant they are formed.

Neutrinos are not photons, however, for the two have quite different properties. Photons interact very easily with particles of matter and are slowed down and absorbed (sometimes very quickly) when they pass through matter.

Neutrinos, however, hardly interact with particles of matter at all and can pass through whole light-years of solid lead without being much affected.

It seems clear, then, that if neutrinos have a rest mass of zero, they are not matter. On the other hand, it takes energy to form them and they carry energy off with them when they leave — so they *are* a form of energy.

Still, they pass through any matter that exists with scarcely any interaction at all; so they do virtually no work. That makes them different from any other form of energy. Perhaps we had better just call them — neutrinos.

64

How does a bubble chamber work?

A bubble chamber is a device for the detection of subatomic particles. It was invented in 1952 by the American physicist Donald A. Glaser, who received the 1960 Nobel Prize in physics as a result.

Essentially, it is a container of liquid at a temperature above its boiling point. The liquid is under pressure so that it is kept from actually boiling. If the pressure is lowered, however, the liquid can boil and bubbles of vapor appear in it.

Suppose that a subatomic particle, such as a proton or a meson, plunges through the liquid in such a bubble chamber. It collides with atoms and molecules in the liquid, and transfers some of its energy to them. There is then a line of atoms and molecules in the liquid that is somewhat hotter than those elsewhere. If the pressure on the liquid is released, the bubbles of vapor form first along the line of energy left in the wake of the subatomic particle. There is thus a visible trail of bubbles marking the passage of the particles, and this is easily photographed.

This visible trail tells physicists a great deal, particularly if the bubble chamber is placed between the poles of a powerful magnet. Those particles capable of leaving a trail of bubbles always carry an electric charge, either positive or negative. If they carry a positive charge, their path curves in one direction under the influence of the magnet; if they carry a negative charge, their path curves in the other. From the sharpness or shallowness of the curve, the physicist can determine the speed of travel. From that, from the thickness of the trail, and so on, he can determine the particles' mass.

When a particle breaks down to two or more particles, the trail branches. In case of collision, there are also branches. In a particular bubble chamber picture, there will be numerous trails, meeting, separating, branching off. Sometimes there is a gap between portions of the trail pattern, and that gap must be filled by some uncharged particle; for uncharged particles, in their travels through the bubble chamber, do not leave tracks.

To the nuclear physicist, the complicated combination of tracks is as meaningful as animal tracks in the snow are to an experienced hunter. From the nature of the tracks, the physicist can identify the particles involved or tell if he has come across a new kind of particle altogether.

Glaser's original bubble chamber was only a few inches in diameter, but now monster chambers many feet in diameter and containing hundreds of gallons of liquid are built.

The liquids used in bubble chambers may be of various kinds. Some contain liquefied noble gases, such as xenon or helium. Others contain liquefied organic gases.

The most useful liquid for bubble chambers, however, is liquid hydrogen. Hydrogen is made up of the simplest atoms known. Each hydrogen atom consists of a nucleus made up of a single proton, circling which is a single electron. Liquid hydrogen is therefore made up of isolated protons and electrons only. All other liquids have atomic nuclei that are conglomerations of several protons, and of several neutrons as well.

The subatomic events that go on within liquid hydrogen are therefore particularly simple, and are all the easier to read from the bubble tracks.

65

What's a breeder reactor?

Uranium-235 is a practical nuclear fuel. That is, slow neutrons will cause uranium-235 atoms to undergo fission (break in two) and produce more slow neutrons which will bring about further atomic fission and so on. Uranium-233 and plutonium-239 are practical nuclear fuels for the same reason.

Unfortunately, uranium-233 and plutonium-239 exist in nature only in the barest traces, and uranium-235, though it does exist in appreciable quantities, is still rather rare. In any sample of natural uranium, only seven atoms out of a thousand are uranium-235. The rest are uranium-238.

Uranium-238, the common variety of uranium, is *not* a practical nuclear fuel. It can be made to undergo fission but only by fast neutrons. The uranium-238 atoms that break in two produce slow neutrons and these do not suffice to bring about further fissions. Uranium-238 can be compared to damp wood, which may be set afire but will eventually fizzle out.

However, suppose uranium-235 is separated from uranium-238 (a rather difficult job) and is used to set up a nuclear reactor. The uranium-235 atoms that form the fuel of the reactor undergo fission and send out vast myriads of slow neutrons in all directions. If the reactor is surrounded by a shell of ordinary uranium (which is mostly uranium-238), the neutrons entering that shell will be absorbed by the uranium-

238. The neutrons cannot force the uranium-238 to undergo fission, but they will bring about other changes which, in the end, will produce plutonium-239. If this plutonium-239 is separated from the uranium (a rather easy job), it can be used as a practical nuclear fuel.

A nuclear reactor that breeds new fuel in this manner to replace the fuel that is used up is a "breeder reactor." A breeder reactor of the proper design will produce plutonium-239 in quantities greater than the uranium-235 consumed. In this way, all earth's supply of uranium, and not just the rare uranium-235, becomes a potential fuel supply.

Thorium, as it occurs naturally, consists entirely of thorium-232. This, like uranium-238, is not a practical nuclear fuel, since it requires fast neutrons to make it undergo fission.

However, if thorium-232 is placed in a shell around a nuclear reactor, the thorium-232 atoms will absorb neutrons and, without undergoing fission, will eventually become atoms of uranium-233. Since uranium-233 is a practical fuel which can be easily separated from thorium, the result is another form of breeder reactor, one which makes the earth's supply of thorium available as a potential nuclear fuel.

The total quantity of uranium and thorium on earth is about 800 times as great as the supply of uranium-235 alone. This means that the proper use of breeder reactors could increase earth's potential energy supply through nuclear fission power plants 800-fold.

66

How hot must we heat hydrogen and for how long to get a fusion reaction to sustain itself?

As hydrogen is heated to higher and higher temperatures, it loses energy at a faster and faster rate through radiation. On the other hand, as the temperature continues to rise, hydrogen atoms lose their electrons, leaving the naked nuclei to smash together and fuse. Where such fusion takes place, energy is produced. As the temperature continues to go up, more and more energy is produced through fusion.

The amount of energy produced by fusion goes up with temperature at a faster rate than the loss of energy by radiation. At some critical temperature, the energy produced by fusion becomes just as great as that lost through radiation. At this point, the temperature is maintained and the fusion reaction becomes self-sustaining. As long as more hydrogen is fed into such a system, energy will be produced steadily.

The temperature required varies with the type of hydrogen. The most common kind is hydrogen (H) with a nucleus made up of one proton. Then there is heavy hydrogen, or deuterium (D), with a nucleus made up of one proton and one neutron, and radioactive hydrogen, or tritium (T), with a nucleus made up of one proton and two neutrons.

The amount of energy produced at a given temperature by fusions involving D is greater than those involving H, and still greater for those involving T.

Fusions involving only H produce so little energy at given temperatures that a temperature of over a billion degrees C. would be required to keep the reaction going in the laboratory. To be sure, it is H that is being fused in the sun's center, where the temperature is only 15,000,000° C., but at so low a temperature, only a tiny proportion of the hydrogen manages to fuse. There is, however, so vast a quantity of H in the sun that even the tiny proportion that fuses is enough to keep the sun's radiation in being.

The lowest temperature required to ignite a fusion would be for one involving only T; that would require only a few million degrees. Unfortunately, tritium is unstable and hardly occurs in nature at all. It would have to be formed in the laboratory as needed and it would be impossible to keep a fusion reaction going in quantities needed by earth on tritium alone.

The fusion of deuterium has an ignition temperature of 400,000,000° C. Deuterium is stable but rare; only 1 atom of hydrogen out of 6700 is of the deuterium variety. Still, that is not too rare. There is enough deuterium in one gallon of ordinary water to produce as much energy through fusion as would be produced by the burning of 300 gallons of gasoline.

One way of reaching the necessary temperature might be through the addition of just enough tritium to act as a starter. The fusion of deuterium with tritium can be ignited at merely 45,000,000° C. If a little of that can be got going, the rest of the mixture could be heated high enough for the deuterium to ignite on its own.

The length of time the temperature must be maintained depends on the density of the hydrogen. The more atoms per cubic centimeter, the more collisions and the faster the ignition. If there are 10^{15} atoms per cubic centimeter (about a ten-thousandth the number of molecules per cubic centimeter in ordinary air), the temperature would have to be maintained for two seconds.

Of course, the higher the density and the higher the temperature, the harder it is to hold the deuterium together even for the brief space of time necessary to start things. Fusion systems have been slowly improved over the years, but conditions for ignition have still not been attained.

67

How does an electron microscope work?

To answer that, let's first ask the question: How do we decide how large an object is?

Light rays reaching us from the two opposite ends of an object form an angle at our eye. From the size of that angle we can judge the apparent size of an object.

If, however, those light rays pass through a convex lens before reaching our eyes, those rays are bent in such a fashion that the angle formed at our eye is made larger. Therefore, the object we see through the lens seems enlarged, and every portion of it seems enlarged. We have a "magnifying lens."

By using several lenses in combination, it becomes possible to magnify object thousands of times and to see clearly details that would be far too small to see with the unaided eyes. We then have an "optical microscope," one that uses light waves. Through it we can see objects as small as bacteria.

Could we pile lens upon lens and eventually make a microscope that would magnify objects so greatly that we could see objects much smaller than bacteria? Even atoms?

Unfortunately, no. Even if we used perfect lenses in perfect combination we could not. Light consists of waves of a certain length (about 1/50,000 of an inch) and nothing smaller than that will show up clearly. The light waves are big enough to "skip over" anything smaller than themselves.

There are forms of light with much smaller wavelengths than that of ordinary light, to be sure. X rays have wavelengths only a ten-thousandth as long as light. Unfortunately, x rays go right through the things we are trying to see.

However, there are electrons, too. These are particles that also act as waves. They have a wavelength that is about the size of those of x rays, and electrons do not go right through the things we are trying to see.

Suppose a beam of light is cast upon an object. The object absorbs the light and casts a shadow, and we see the object by the comparison of light and shadow. If a beam of electrons is cast upon an object, the object will absorb the electrons and it will cast an "electron shadow." It would be dangerous for us to try to put our eyes in the way of an electron beam, but we can put a photographic film in the way. The electron shadow will show us the shape of the object and even its details if some parts of it absorb electrons more strongly or less strongly than other parts.

But what if the object is very small? If light beams were involved, we could use lenses to bend those beams in such a way as to magnify the appearance of the object. We can't use ordinary lenses to bend an electron beam, but we can use something else. The electrons carry an electric charge and this means that they will follow a curved path in a magnetic field. If a magnetic field of the proper strength and shape is used, a beam of electrons can be manipulated in exactly the same way that a lens will manipulate a beam of light.

In short, we have an "electron microscope," one which makes use of beams of electrons exactly as an "optical microscope" makes use of beams of light.

The difference is that electrons have a wavelength so much shorter than ordinary light that an electron microscope will show us objects as tiny as viruses, where an optical microscope cannot.

68

What is entropy?

Energy can be turned into work only if, within the particular system you are using, there is an unevenness in the concentration of energy. The energy then tends to flow from the point of higher concentration to that of lower concentration until everything is evened out. It is by taking advantage of this flow that you can get work out of energy.

The water at the source of a river is higher and has more gravitational energy than the water at the mouth of the river. For that reason water flows down the river into the ocean. (If it weren't for rainfall, all the water on the continents would flow downhill to the ocean and the ocean level would rise slightly. The total gravitational energy would remain the same but it would be more evenly distributed.)

It is while the water flows downhill that a waterwheel can be made to turn, and work can be done by the water. Water on a single level cannot do work; not even if the water is on a high plateau and has an unusually high gravitational energy. It is the difference in energy concentration and the flow toward evenness that are crucial.

This is true of any kind of energy. In steam engines there is a heat reservoir which turns water into steam and a cold reservoir which condenses the steam to water again. It is this difference in temperature which is crucial. At any single undifferentiated temperature, however high, no work can be obtained.

"Entropy" is a term introduced in 1850 by a German physicist, Rudolf J. E. Clausius, to represent the evenness with which energy of any form is spread out. The more evenly it is spread out, the higher the entropy. If the energy is spread out perfectly evenly, entropy is at a maximum for the system under consideration.

It seemed to Clausius that, left to itself, within a system, the energy differences always tended to even out. If a hot object is placed in contact with a cold object, heat flows in such a way that the hot object cools and the cold object warms until both are at the same temperature. If two water reservoirs are connected and one has a higher water level than the other, gravitational pull will make one water level sink and the other rise, till both levels are even and gravitational energy is smoothed out.

Clausius therefore said that it was a general rule in nature that differences in concentrations of energy tended to equalize. In other words, "Entropy increases with time."

The study of energy flow from point of higher concentration to points of lower concentration was carried out most thoroughly in connection with energy in the form of heat. The study of energy flow and of interchanges of energy and work has therefore come to be known as "thermodynamics," from Greek words meaning "heat motion."

It had already been decided that energy could neither be created nor destroyed. This was so fundamental a rule that it is called the "first law of thermodynamics."

Clausius' suggesting that entropy increased with time seemed almost as fundamental a general rule and it is called the "second law of thermodynamics."

69

Is the universe running down?

According to the "second law of thermodynamics," entropy is always increasing. That means that differences in energy concentration are always evening out. When all differences in energy concentration have evened out completely, no more work can be extracted from energy; no more changes can take place.

Consider a watch. A watch goes because there is a concentration of energy in its mainspring or its battery. As the spring unwinds or the chemical reaction of the battery proceeds, there is a flow of energy from the point of high concentration to the point of low and as a result of this flow the watch goes. Once the spring is entirely unwound or the battery has completed its chemical change, the energy level has evened out throughout the watch, there is no more energy flow, and the watch no longer goes. It has "run down." It is by analogy with this that we say the universe will "run down" when all the energy is completely evened out.

Of course, we can wind up the watch again or buy a new battery. To wind up the watch, we use our own muscle power and we ourselves "run down" a little bit. We can buy a new battery, but that must be manufactured and, to make it, man's industrial establishment must "run down" a little bit.

We can renew our own muscle power by eating, but the food is formed originally by plants that make use of the sun's energy. Man's industrial establishment runs chiefly on coal and oil formed by plants in eons past from the sun's energy. As things "run down" on earth, we can always "wind them up" again by using something that usually stretches back to the sun's energy and the way it is "running down."

The sun is made up largely of hydrogen, which contains much more energy per particle than do more complicated atoms such as helium, oxygen, and iron. Inside the sun, there is a gradual evening out of energy concentration as hydrogen turns into more complicated atoms. (In atomic power plants on earth, the same thing happens as uranium atoms turn into less complicated atoms. If we ever develop hydrogen fusion plants, we will be duplicating, in a way, what is going on in the sun.)

Eventually, as far as we can tell now, energy concentrations will even out in the sun and leave it with intermediate-sized atoms only. This will be true also of all the other stars in the universe and of everything in the universe.

If the second law of thermodynamics is true, then all energy concentrations everywhere in the universe are evening out and the universe is, in that sense, running down. If it is true, then entropy will reach a maximum when all the energy of the universe is perfectly evened out and then nothing more will happen because though the energy will still be all there, there will no longer be any flow to make things happen.

Depressing (*if* the second law is actually true under all conditions), but there is no need for immediate alarm. The process will take many trillions of years to reach its end, and the universe as it now exists will not only last our time but, in all probability, it will last mankind's time and even the earth's time.

70

What is the connection between entropy and order?

I magine nine people arranged in a square — three rows of three, all the rows and columns evenly spaced. We can call this an orderly arrangement because it is neat and symmetrical and is easily described.

If every one of the nine men takes one step forward simultaneously, they will remain in formation and the arrangement will still be orderly. The same is true if each takes a step backward, or each a step to the left, or each a step to the right.

Suppose, however, each man is told to take one step, either forward, backward, right, or left, and each man is completely free to choose his direction. It may be that each man will independently just happen to decide to step forward one step. In that case, order will be maintained.

However, the chance that a particular man will step forward is only 1 out of 4, since he is free to move in any of four different directions. The chance that all nine men will independently choose to move forward is 1 out of $4 \times 4 \times 4 \times 4 \times 4 \times 4 \times 4 \times 4 \times 4$, or 1 out of 262,144.

If all move right, or all left, or all back, they also keep in order so that the total chance of doing so is 4 out of 262,144, or 1 out of 65,538. Even so, you can see what a tiny chance order has, and you know that if the men are given freedom to move, then a single step will be enough to break the square and decrease the amount of order. Even if by some freak of chance they do all move together, then the next step will, in all probability, break the square.

140

This is the case where only nine men are involved and where only four different directions of movement are allowed. In most natural processes, we deal with uncounted trillions of atoms free to move in very many different ways. If, by some chance, there were some sort of order imposed on the arrangement of atoms to begin with, then any free random motion, any spontaneous change, would be bound to decrease that order, or, to put it another way, increase disorder.

According to the second law of thermodynamics, the entropy of the universe is always increasing; that is, the energy distribution in the universe is constantly evening out. It can be shown that any process which evens out energy concentration also increases disorder. Therefore, this tendency to increase disorder in the universe with the free random motions of the particles making it up is but another aspect of the second law, and entropy can be considered a measure of the disorder present in the universe.

If we look at it this way, we can see the workings of the second law all about us, since natural changes clearly work in the direction of disorder and it is only with special effort, at a cost to ourselves, that we restore order. Our belongings get out of place, our houses get messy, our clothes get dirty, and we must constantly straighten and dust and clean to remain in one place. It may make us feel better to think that this is the result of the working out of a great cosmic law — but somehow it doesn't in my case.

71

What is the connection between entropy and time?

Suppose we consider a motion picture of the earth going around the sun, taken from far off in space, and speed it up so that we can see the earth seem to race along in its orbit. Suppose we run the film first forward, then backward. Can we tell which is which just by looking at the earth as it moves?

You might say that the earth moves about the sun in a counterclockwise direction as seen from above the sun's north pole. If it seems to move in a clockwise direction, then we know that the film is running backward and that therefore time is running backward.

But, then, if you view the earth moving about the sun from above the sun's south pole, earth moves about the sun in a clockwise direction. How can you tell, if you see that clockwise direction, whether you are above the north pole with time running backward or above the south pole with time running forward?

You can't. In very simple processes involving only a few objects, it is impossible to tell whether time is moving forward or backward. The laws of nature hold equally in either case. This is also true if you consider subatomic particles.

An electron curving in a certain way with time moving forward might, for all you know, be a positron curving in that way with time moving backward. If you consider that particle only, you can't possibly determine which alternative is correct.

In these very simple processes in which you cannot tell whether time is moving forward or backward, there is no entropy change (or one so small it can be ignored). In ordinary processes involving many particles, on the other hand, entropy always increases. This is the same as saying that disorder always increases. A diver drops into the pool and water splashes upward; a vase falls and breaks; leaves fall from a tree and scatter on the ground.

All these things and everything else that happens ordinarily about us can be shown to involve an increase in entropy. We are used to seeing entropy increase and we accept that increase as indicating that everything is going normally and that we are moving forward in time. If suddenly we were to see entropy decreasing, the only way we could explain it would be to suppose that we were moving backward in time.

For instance, suppose we were viewing a film made of everyday activities. Suppose we saw a water splash gathering together and a diver rising upward to a diving board. Suppose we saw the fragments of a vase come together and rise through the air back to a position on a table. Suppose we saw leaves gather themselves up from the ground and rise back to specific attachments on a tree. All these things show a decrease in entropy and we know that this is so completely out of the order of things that the film must be running backward. In fact, so queerly do events take place when time runs backward that the sight makes us laugh.

Entropy is sometimes called "time's arrow," in consequence, because its steady increase marks what we consider to be the "forward direction" for time. (Mind you, if all the atoms within objects moved in just the right way, all these backward things *could* happen, but the chances of that are so small that we can quite ignore the possibility.)

72

If the universe is constantly running down, how did it get wound up to begin with?

The best answer one can give to that question is that no one knows. As far as we can tell, all changes are in the direction of increasing entropy, of increasing disorder, of increasing randomness, of running down. Yet the universe was once in a position from which it could run down for trillions of years. How did it get into that position?

I can think of three possible answers, all of which are only speculations:

1) We don't know all the kinds of things that are happening in the universe. The changes we do observe are all in the direction of increasing entropy. Somewhere, though, there may be changes under unusual conditions that we can't as yet study which are in the direction of decreasing entropy. In that case, the universe may be standing still on the whole. It is only the small part we can observe that seems to be running downhill and elsewhere there is a balancing movement uphill.

2) Suppose that the universe experiences no decrease in entropy anywhere and that it *does* run downhill all the way. At maximum entropy, all the energy in the universe is spread out evenly and there is no further progression of time in either direction. But all the energy is still there and all the atoms of the universe possess some of that energy and are moving randomly.

It may be, then, that through sheer random movement, a certain amount of energy concentration is piled into part of the universe. By random motion, a certain amount of order is produced once more. Once that happens, that part of the universe begins to run down again.

It may be that entropy maximum is the normal condition of a vast infinite universe and that every once in a long while (as time is ordinarily measured) small parts of it gain some order and that we are in such a small part now.

3) Perhaps the only reason entropy seems to be increasing steadily in the universe is that the universe happens to be expanding. Under this condition only, then, might disorderly arrangements be more probable than orderly ones.

There are some astronomers who suspect that the universe will not expand forever. An initial explosion hurled it apart but the mutual gravitational attraction of its parts may be gradually decreasing its rate of expansion, may make it come to a halt, and may then slowly force it to begin contracting again. It may be that in a contracting universe, more orderly arrangements become more probable than less orderly ones. That means that there will be a natural change in the direction of greater order and therefore a continual decrease in entropy.

If that is so, the universe may be running down as it expands and then winding up again as it contracts, and it may be doing this over and over through all eternity.

We might even combine speculations 1 and 3 if we consider the "black holes." These are regions in which mass is so concentrated and gravity so powerful that everything falls in and nothing, not even light, comes out. They are tiny samples of contracting universe; perhaps in those black holes the second law (of thermodynamics) is reversed, and while the universe runs down in most places it is gradually being wound up there.

73

Radio waves as well as light waves are used to "see" things in space. Are there other kinds of waves we can "see" with?

Radio waves are related to light waves, the difference being primarily a matter of length; radio waves are much longer than light waves.

There is a whole family of waves of varying length, referred to as the electromagnetic spectrum. This spectrum is usually divided into seven regions which, in order of decreasing length of waves, may be listed as: 1) radio waves, 2) microwaves, 3) infrared rays, 4) visible light, 5) ultraviolet rays, 6) x rays, and 7) gamma rays.

Earth's atmosphere is reasonably transparent only to visible light and to microwaves. Other portions of the electromagnetic spectrum are almost entirely absorbed long before they have passed through the air. If we observe the heavens from the earth's surface, then, it is only light and microwaves that are useful to us.

Mankind has been observing the heavens by means of light from the very beginning, for men have always had eyes. It was not until 1931, however, that an American engineer, Karl Jansky, first discovered that he was detecting microwaves emitted by heavenly bodies. Since microwaves are sometimes viewed as very short radio waves, this branch of astronomical observation is called "radio astronomy."

Some objects which can be detected by their microwave emission do not emit very much light. In other words, some radio sources are invisible to the sight.

Once observations are made from outside the atmosphere, however, the entire electromagnetic spectrum becomes available for study.

Rocket observations have made it clear that the heavenly bodies bombard earth with radiation of all sorts. The study of this radiation could well increase our knowledge of the universe by a great deal.

There are regions in the sky, for instance, which emit ultraviolet light in considerable quantity. The Orion nebula is an ultraviolet source, and so are the regions about the first-magnitude star Spica. Why ultraviolet light should originate in such quantities in those regions is not yet known.

Even more mysterious is the fact that there are a number of spots in the sky that have been discovered to serve as rich sources of x rays. In order to emit x rays, an object must be incredibly hot; a million degrees or more. No ordinary star is that hot on the surface. But there are neutron stars in which matter is packed so tightly that all the mass in an object the size of the sun would be squeezed into a ball only ten miles across. These and other strange objects may emit x rays.

Astronomers probably won't be able to make thorough studies of the various kinds of radiation reaching us from space until they can get their observatories permanently beyond the atmosphere.

The moon, with its lack of atmosphere, would be an ideal place for such an observatory. The possibility of building such observatories, and of increasing our knowledge of the universe vastly in this way, is one of the most attractive reasons we have for trying to reach and colonize the moon.

74

As a substance is heated, it glows red, then orange, then yellow. But then it becomes white. Why doesn't it go through the spectrum and become green hot?

Any object, at any energy higher than absolute zero, radiates electromagnetic waves. If its temperature is very low, it radiates only long radio waves, very low in energy. As the temperature goes up, it radiates more and more of such waves, but it also begins to radiate shorter (and more energetic) radio waves as well. As the temperature continues to rise, the still more energetic microwaves begin to be radiated, and then infrared.

This doesn't mean that *only* long radio waves are radiated at one temperature, and *only* short ones at a higher temperature, then *only* microwaves, and *only* infrared. Actually, the entire range of radiation is radiated. There is, however, a peak radiation; a range of wavelengths that is most radiated, with smaller amounts on the low-energy side of the peak and still smaller amounts on the high-energy side.

By the time the object becomes as warm as the human body (37° C.), the peak of the radiation is in the long infrared. The human body is still radiating radio waves as well, but the shortest and most energetic wavelengths are always the most easily detectable and therefore the most prominent.

Once the temperature reaches about 600° C., the peak radiation is in the short-wave infrared. By that time, however, the small quantity of radiation on the high-energy side of the peak becomes particularly significant, for it reaches into the region of visible red light. The object therefore glows a deep red.

This red is only a small percentage of the total radiation but we happen to be able to see it and therefore give it all our attention and say that the body is "red hot."

With still rising temperature, the peak radiation continues to shift toward the shorter wavelengths and more and more visible light at shorter and shorter wavelengths is given off. Though more red light is radiated, orange and yellow light are added in smaller, but significant quantities. By the time 1000° C. is reached, the mixture of colors impresses our eye as orange, and by 2000° C. the mixture impresses it as yellow. This doesn't mean that *only* orange light is radiated at 1000° C. and only yellow at 2000° C. If that were the case we would indeed expect "green heat" to follow. But we are seeing *mixtures* of light.

By the time 6000° C. is reached (the surface temperature of our sun), the peak radiation is in the visible yellow and we are getting large quantities of visible light all the way from violet to red. The entire range of visible light impresses our eye as white so that the sun is "white hot."

For objects still hotter than the sun, all the wavelengths of visible light continue to be radiated and in even greater quantities. The peak radiation moves into the blue, however, so that the mixture becomes unbalanced to our eyes and the white has a bluish tinge added.

All this is for heated objects that give off "continuous spectra" radiating light as a broad band of wavelengths. Certain substances under the proper conditions will radiate light in only certain wavelengths. Barium nitrate will radiate green light when it is heated and is used in fireworks for that purpose. That is "green heat," if you like.

75

What is polarized light?

Light can be looked upon as made up of tiny waves, and these waves can oscillate in any plane. In a particular beam of light some waves might be oscillating up and down, some from side to side, and some in various diagonal directions. The direction of oscillation might be spread evenly all around, with no one plane being favored or having much more than its even share of light waves. Ordinary light from the sun or from an electric bulb is like this.

Suppose, though, that light travels through a transparent crystal. The crystal is made up of various atoms or groups of atoms lined up in regular rows and sheets. A light wave would find it easy to get through the crystal if it happens to be oscillating in a plane that manages to snake it between two sheets of atoms. If it were oscillating in a plane at an angle to that, it would hit the atoms and much of its energy would go into making them vibrate. Such light would be partly or entirely absorbed.

(You can get an idea of what this is like if you imagine one end of a rope tied to a tree in a neighbor's yard and the other end held in your hand. Suppose the rope passed between two pickets of a fence about halfway. If you made waves up and down, those waves would pass between the pickets and travel from you to the tree. The fence would be "transparent" to those waves. If you made waves right and left, they would hit the pickets and wouldn't pass through.)

Some crystals force all the energy of light waves into two separate rays. The plane of oscillation is no longer spread evenly. In one ray, all the waves oscillate in one particular plane and, in the other, they oscillate in a plane at right angles to the first. No diagonal oscillations are possible.

150

When light waves are forced to oscillate in one particular plane, such light is said to be "plane-polarized" or simply "polarized." Ordinary light oscillating in any direction is "unpolarized."

Why "polarized"? When the phenomenon was first given a name back in 1808, the French engineer E. L. Malus, who invented the name, had a mistaken theory about the nature of light. He thought light was made up of particles with poles like those on a magnet. He thought the light emerging from the crystal might have all the poles in one direction. That proved wrong, but the name was too firmly accepted to change.

When a crystal produces two rays of light, each with a different plane of polarization, the two have somewhat different properties. They may bend by different amounts in passing through the crystal. A crystal can be so devised that one ray is reflected away and only the other gets all the way through.

In the case of some crystals, only one ray gets through because the other is absorbed and turned into heat. Polaroid glasses (which have tiny crystals of this sort embedded in plastic) absorb much of the light in this way, and absorb more because of the tinting. In this way, they cut down glare.

When polarized light passes through a solution containing certain kinds of asymmetric molecules, the plane of its oscillation is twisted. From the direction and amount of the twist, chemists have been able to make many deductions about the actual structure of molecules, particularly organic ones. Polarized light has thus been enormously important to chemical theory.

76

Can light exert a force on matter?

A beam of light contains energy and, when it strikes an opaque object and is absorbed, something has to happen to the energy. Most of it is converted to heat; that is, the particles making up the opaque object gain the light energy and begin to vibrate more rapidly.

However, can the beam of light exert a direct force on the opaque object? Can it impart its motion to the object absorbing it? The effect of a massive body in motion on anything that gets in its way is clear. A bowling ball will hit a tenpin and send it flying. But light is made up of particles of zero mass. Can it nevertheless transfer its motion and exert a force on matter?

Back in 1873, the Scottish physicist J. Clerk Maxwell studied the problem theoretically. He showed that light, even if it were composed of massless waves, would still exert force on matter. The quantity of the force would depend on the energy contained in the moving beam of light *per unit length*. There is the catch. Suppose you had a flashlight that you turned on for just one second. The light it emits in that second contains considerable energy, but in that one second the first bit of light emitted has moved 186,282 miles. All the light put out in one second by the flash of light is stretched into a beam that long, and the amount of energy in one foot of it, or even one mile, is tiny indeed.

It is for that reason we are not aware of any force exerted by light on matter under ordinary circumstances.

Suppose, though, you were to take a light horizontal rod with flat disks at each end and suspend that rod, at its center, by a thin quartz thread. The slightest force on one disk would cause the rod to twist about the quartz thread. If a beam of light shone on one of the disks, the rod would rotate if that beam exerted a force.

Naturally, the tiny force would be masked if there were the slightest wind pushing against the disks, so the whole system has to be enclosed in a chamber. Even the bouncing of air molecules off the disk would create forces much greater than that of light, so the chamber must be highly evacuated. Once that is done and certain other precautions are taken, it might be possible to measure the small shift in the position of the disk when a strong light beam is made to shine on it.

In 1901, two American physicists, Ernest F. Nichols and Gordon F. Hull, carried through such an experiment at Dartmouth College and showed that light did indeed exert a force, and by just about the amount predicted by Maxwell twenty-eight years before. At almost the same time, a Russian physicist, Peter N. Lebedev, using a somewhat more complicated setup, proved the same thing.

Once the existence of this "radiation pressure" was demonstrated, astronomers were sure it explained something interesting about comets. The tail of a comet always points away from the sun, streaming behind the comet as it approaches the sun. The tail swings about as the comet moves around the sun at its closest approach. Then, when the comet is moving away from the sun, the tail precedes it.

"Aha," thought the astronomers. "Radiation pressure!"

For a half-century, they were confident this was so, but they were wrong. The radiation pressure of sunlight isn't strong enough and it is the solar wind that pushes comet tails away from the sun.

77

Red light is least changed in passing through
a prism, most changed in passing through a
diffraction grating. Why the difference?

Light can be viewed as a wave motion, and ordinary sunlight is a collection of waves of different lengths. Light of different wavelengths produces different effects on our retinas, and it is those which give us our sensation of color. Of visible forms of light, red light has the longest wavelength; then orange, yellow, green, blue, and, finally, with the shortest wavelength, violet.

When light passes from air into glass, water, or other transparent media, it slows down. If a beam of light approaches a piece of glass at an oblique angle from the right, the right side of the beam, which strikes the glass first, is slowed down first. For an instant, the right side is moving slowly while the left side continues at full speed, and the result is that the beam changes direction as it enters the glass. This is "refraction."

The same thing would happen if a column of soldiers were to march obliquely from a paved highway into a plowed field. The soldiers on the side of the column toward the field would reach it first and be slowed down first, and unless a conscious effort were made to prevent it, the column would shift direction as it entered the field.

The slowing effect of the field is produced by the difficulty of pulling one's legs out of the soft soil. Once free, the leg moves through the air above as quickly over the field as over the highway. This means that a long-legged soldier, who makes fewer contacts with the ground in a given distance, thanks to his long stride, than a short-legged soldier does, is slowed less. A column of long-legged soldiers would have their direction of march changed less than would a column of short-legged soldiers.

The long-wave red light is similar, in this respect, to a long-legged

soldier. It is slowed less than any other kind of visible light and is, therefore, refracted least. Violet light is, of course, refracted most.

Diffraction involves a completely different principle. A wave motion can freely move around an obstacle that is no larger than the length of one of its waves. The larger the obstacle, the less freely it can move around them.

The wavelengths of light are so tiny (about 1/50,000 of an inch long) that light does not bend noticeably about ordinary obstructions but continues on in a straight line past them and produces sharp shadows. (Sound waves, which are entirely different in nature from light waves, are much longer. That is why you can hear around a corner, but can't see around one — at least, not without mirrors.)

A diffraction grating consists of a large number of very fine opaque lines drawn parallel to each other against a transparent background. The opaque lines are fine enough so that even the tiny light waves, passing through the transparent regions nearby, can slip around them a little. This is "diffraction."

Clearly, the longer the wavelength of light, the smaller the obstruction of the opaque lines and the farther that light can reach around it. The long-wave red light can reach farthest around the opaque lines and is therefore diffracted most. Violet light is, of course, diffracted least.

Both a refracting prism and a diffraction grating will yield a "rainbow" or spectrum. One spectrum is, however, the reverse of the other. Reading outward from the original line of direction of light, the refraction spectrum is: red, orange, yellow, green, blue, and violet. The diffraction spectrum is: violet, blue, green, yellow, orange, red.

78

What happens to the energy when two light beams interfere and produce darkness?

A light beam may be thought of as consisting of a train of waves. If two light beams meet at a small angle, it is possible that the waves of one may meet the waves of another in such a way that one wave is moving up just where the other is moving down, and vice versa. The two waves "interfere" and cancel each other out partly, or even entirely. The result is that a combination of two waves can, in this way, produce a less intense light than either wave alone would.

But each set of waves represents a certain amount of energy. If one wave cancels the other, producing darkness where light existed before, does that mean the energy has disappeared?

Certainly not! One of the fundamental rules of physics is that energy *cannot* cease to exist. This is the "law of conservation of energy." In interference, some energy has ceased to exist *in the form of light.* A precisely equal amount of energy must come into existence in some other form.

The least organized form of energy is that of the random motion of the particles making up matter, and this we call "heat." Energy tends to lose organization when it changes form, so that when energy seems to disappear it is best to search for heat, for molecules moving randomly at greater velocities than before.

This is true in the case of light interference. You might, in theory, so arrange two light beams as to make them interfere perfectly. The two will then fall on a screen and leave it completely dark. In that case, the screen will nevertheless grow warmer. The energy has not gone, it has merely changed its form.

A similar problem is this. Suppose you wind up the mainspring of a clock tightly. It now contains more energy than the same spring unwound. Suppose, next, you dissolve the wound mainspring in acid. What happens to the energy?

Again it is turned into heat. If you begin with two acid solutions at equal temperature and dissolve an unwound mainspring in one and a wound mainspring (otherwise identical) in the other, the solution that has dissolved the wound mainspring would be warmer than the solution that has dissolved the unwound one.

It was only in 1847, after physicists thoroughly appreciated the nature of heat, that the law of conservation of energy was understood.

Since then, by adhering to the law, new understanding of basic phenomena has been achieved. For instance, in radioactive transformations more heat is produced than can be accounted for by nineteenth-century physical calculations. That problem was solved when Einstein worked out his famous $e = mc^2$ equation, showing that matter itself was a form of energy.

Again, in some radioactive transformations, electrons are produced with too little energy. Rather than admit a violation of the law of conservation of energy, Wolfgang Pauli, in 1931, suggested that another particle, the neutrino, was also produced and that the neutrino carried off the rest of the energy. And he was right.

79

What is the Coriolis effect?

If an object is stationary or is moving at a constant velocity relative to some fixed point, then there is no problem in moving across that object. If you wish to travel from point A at one edge to point B at the other, in a straight line, then you can do so without feeling any difficulty in the process.

If, however, different parts of an object are moving at different velocities, the situation is quite otherwise. Consider a merry-go-round, or any large flat object rotating about its center. The entire object rotates in one piece, but a point near the center marks out a small circle and is moving slowly, while a point near the outer edge marks out a large circle and is therefore moving rapidly.

Suppose you are at a point near the center and wish to walk out toward a point near the outer edge, in a straight line directly away from the center. At your starting point near the center you partake of the velocity of that point and are moving slowly. As you move outward, however, the effect of inertia is to keep you moving slowly, but the ground under your feet is moving faster and faster, the further you step outward. The combination of your slowness and the ground's fastness causes you to feel pushed in the direction opposite the motion of rotation. If the merry-go-round is moving in a counterclockwise direction, you find your pathway curving more and more sharply clockwise as you move outward.

If you start at a point near the outer edge and move inward, you retain the fast motion of your starting point but the ground under you is moving more and more slowly. You feel yourself pushed, therefore, farther and farther in the direction of the rotation. If the merry-go-round is moving in a counterclockwise direction, you are again curving more and more sharply clockwise.

If you start at a point near the center, move to a point near the outer edge, then back to a point near the center, and follow the path of least resistance, you will find that you have taken a roughly circular path.

This phenomenon was first studied in detail in 1835 by a French physicist, Gaspard de Coriolis, and it is called the "Coriolis effect" as a result. Sometimes it is called the "Coriolis force," but it is not really a force; it is simply the result of inertia.

The most important consequence of the Coriolis effect in everyday affairs involves the rotating earth. A point on the surface of the earth at the equator sweeps out a large circle in twenty-four hours and therefore moves quickly. The farther north (or south) we go from the equator, the smaller the circle swept out by a surface point in one day and the more slowly it moves.

A wind, or an ocean current, heading northward from the tropics, is moving very rapidly from west to east, with the earth's rotation, to begin with. As it travels northward, it maintains its velocity, but the earth's surface is moving at a less and less rapid rate, so that the wind or the current outraces it and begins to curve toward the east more and more. In the end, winds and currents move in large circles — clockwise in the Northern Hemisphere and counterclockwise in the Southern Hemisphere.

It is the Coriolis effect which starts the curving motion that, when concentrated more tightly (and therefore more energetically), becomes a hurricane, or, still more tightly and energetically, a tornado.

80

Sound travels faster through dense substances like water or steel than through air; yet it travels faster in warm air than in cold air, and warm air is less dense than cold air. Is this a paradox?

What our ears detect as sound is caused by a vibration that brings about an oscillating movement in the atoms or molecules making up the medium through which sound travels. The vibration pushes nearby molecules together, compressing them. The compressed molecules move apart, bringing about a compression in a neighboring region, so that the area of compression seems to travel outward from the sound source. The speed at which the wave of compression moves outward from the source is the speed of sound in that medium.

The speed of sound depends upon the natural speed with which the molecules making up a substance move. Once a particular section of air, for instance, is compressed, the molecules move apart again because of their natural random motions. If this random motion is fast, the molecules of the compressed section move apart quickly and compress the molecules of the neighboring section quickly. The neighboring section also moves apart quickly and compresses the next section quickly. On the whole, then, the wave of compression moves outward quickly and so the speed of sound is high.

Anything which increases (or decreases) the natural speed of the molecules of air will increase (or decrease) the speed of sound in air.

As it happens, air molecules move more rapidly at higher temperatures than at lower ones. For that reason sound travels more rapidly through warm air than through cold air. This has nothing to do with density.

160

At 32° F., the freezing point of water, sound travels at 743 miles per hour. This speed goes up about 0.7 miles per hour with each Fahrenheit-degree rise in temperature.

Generally, gases made up of lighter molecules than those of air are less dense than air. The lighter molecules also move more quickly. The speed of sound through such light gases is faster than in air, not because of any change in density, but because of the faster motion of the molecules. Sound travels at 2900 miles per hour in hydrogen at 32° F.

When we come to liquids and solids, the situation is quite different from that in gases. In gases, molecules are very far apart and scarcely interfere with each other. If molecules are pushed closer together, they move farther apart through random motions only. In liquids and solids, however, atoms and molecules are in contact. If they are pushed together, their mutual repulsion forces them apart again very quickly.

This is especially true of solids, where atoms and molecules are held more or less rigidly in place. The more rigidly they are held, the more rapidly they spring back when pushed together. For this reason, sound travels more rapidly through liquids than through gases; still more rapidly through solids; most rapidly through rigid solids. Density is not the basic reason.

Thus, sound travels through water at a speed of about 3300 mph and through steel at a speed of about 11,000 mph.

81

Do ships sink all the way to the bottom of the sea, or does the pressure hold them up in deep water when they go down so far?

An object will sink in water if it is denser than water. The density of water is one gram per cubic centimeter, and such substances as rock and metal are considerably denser than that. Ships built of huge masses of steel float because they enclose large volumes of air. The average density of the steel and other construction materials, plus the volume of air inside the ship, is less than that of water. If through some accident water is allowed to enter the ship, the average density of construction material plus the contained water is greater than that of water alone and the ship sinks.

As it sinks, the object is subjected to greater and greater pressures. At the surface of the ocean, the pressure (due to the atmosphere) is 14.7 pounds per square inch of surface. Thirty-three feet below the surface, the weight of that depth of water adds another 14.7 pounds per square inch to the pressure. Each additional depth of thirty-three feet adds another 14.7 pounds per square inch, and at the bottom of the deepest know portion of the ocean floor, the pressure is about 1100 times atmospheric pressure. That comes to about eight tons per square inch.

Such high pressures have no effect whatever on "holding up" sinking objects. The pressure is exerted equally in all directions, down and sideways just as much as up, so that the object continues sinking quite oblivious to any rise in pressure.

But there is another factor. Pressure will compress water, increasing its density. Can water become so dense as a result of great pressure that objects will stop sinking and float on the denser deep-sea water?

No! The compression effect is very small. Even at a pressure of 8

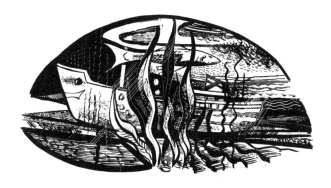

tons per square inch, the density of water rises only from 1.00 to about 1.05 grams per cubic centimeter. If a solid had a density of 1.02 grams per cubic centimeter, it would indeed sink beneath the surface waters and come to a floating halt about three miles down, then sink no further. Ordinary structural materials, however, have densities considerably higher than 1.05. Aluminum and steel have densities of 2.7 and 7.8 grams per cubic centimeter, respectively. Metal ships would sink to the bottom of the ocean's deepest abyss without the slightest chance of floating.

But suppose the ocean were deeper still. Would a time ever come when a bar of aluminum, say, might reach a maximum depth? The answer is still No!

If the oceans were about forty-two miles deep (instead of seven at most) the pressure at the bottom would rise to some 45 tons per square inch and the density of water to about 1.3 grams per cubic centimeter. At that point, however, the water would no longer remain liquid but would be converted into a solid substance called "Ice VI." (Ice VI is denser than water, whereas "Ice I" — ordinary ice — is less dense than water.)

Aluminum, therefore, and any other substance with a density greater than 1.3 grams per cubic centimeter, would continue falling through any depth of ocean just as long as the water of the ocean remained liquid and would eventually come to rest on a solid surface of either ordinary ocean bottom or Ice VI. Liquid water would never become dense enough to float solid aluminum, let alone solid steel.

82

Which are the most active chemical elements, and why?

Electrons surround the nucleus of an atom in concentric spheres called "shells." For each element there are a fixed number of electrons in each shell. The arrangement is particularly stable when eight electrons are present in the outermost shell.

Suppose, though, that an element has so many electrons that when eight of them are placed in one of the outer shells, there remain a few extra electrons that have to be placed by themselves in a shell still farther out. These few outermost electrons (negatively charged) are only weakly held by the positively charged atomic nucleus at the center of the cell. The outermost electrons are easily given up to other atoms, so that what is left of the atom now has that stable arrangement of eight electrons in the outermost shell.

Chemical reactions involve the transfer of electrons, so an element that can easily lose one or more electrons will easily engage in such reactions and is "chemically active." Generally, the fewer the number of electrons over the eight, the more easily they are transferred and the more active the element. The most active elements are therefore those with a single electron over the eight — those in which the single electron is all by itself in the outermost shells.

Examples of such elements are sodium, with an electron arrangement in three shells (2, 8, 1), and potassium, with an electron arrangement in four shells (2, 8, 8, 1).

The inner shells of electrons tend to insulate that lone outermost electron from the positively charged nucleus. The more shells there are in between, the weaker the hold of the nucleus on the outermost electron and the easier it is for the atom to transfer it. Thus, potassium is more active than sodium, and cesium (2, 8, 18, 18, 8, 1) is even more active.

More active still would be francium (2, 8, 18, 32, 18, 8, 1), but only a few atoms of that can be studied at a time. Even its most stable isotope has a half-life of only twenty-one minutes. Cesium is therefore the most active *stable* metallic element.

Suppose, now, that an element has just too few electrons to make up an outermost shell of eight. Such atoms have tendencies to accept several electrons to make up the necessary eight. They therefore engage in chemical reactions and are active.

Generally, the fewer the number of electrons required to make up the eight, the greater the tendency to accept electrons. The most active elements of this kind, therefore, are those with atoms containing seven electrons in the outermost shell, and needing only *one* electron to make up the eight.

Examples of such elements are chlorine, the atoms of which have an electron arrangement of 2, 8, 7, and bromine, with 2, 8, 18, 7.

In the case of such elements, the stronger the pull of the nucleus, the greater the tendency to pull in that missing electron. The fewer the number of inner shells of electrons, the less insulation there is about the nucleus, the stronger the pull of that nucleus, and the more active the element.

Of the elements of this type, the one with the smallest number of shells of electrons is fluorine, with an electron arrangement of 2, 7. Fluorine is therefore the most active of all nonmetallic elements.

83

What is so noble about the noble gases?

Elements which react with difficulty or not at all with other elements are called "inert." Nitrogen and platinum are examples of inert elements.

In the 1890s, a number of gases were discovered in the atmosphere which did not seem to engage in any chemical reactions at all. These new gases — helium, neon, argon, krypton, xenon, and radon — are more inert than any other elements and are grouped together as the "inert gases."

Inert elements are sometimes called "noble" because they did not react with other elements and this seemed a kind of aristocratic stand-offishness on their parts. Gold and platinum are examples of "noble metals," and the inert gases were sometimes called the "noble gases," for this reason. Until 1962, "inert gas" was the more common phrase, perhaps because "noble gas" seemed unfitting for democratic societies.

The reason the inert gases are inert rests in the fact that the number of electrons each contains are arranged in shells in such a way that every shell has a particularly stable number. In particular, the outermost shell has eight electrons. Thus, the electron arrangement in neon is 2, 8, and in argon is 2, 8, 8. To add or subtract electrons breaks up this stable arrangement and therefore no electron changes take place. This means that chemical reactions don't take place and the elements are inert.

The extent of the inertness, however, depends on the strength with which the positively charged nucleus at the center of the atom holds on to the eight electrons in the outermost shell. The more electron shells there are between the outermost and the center, the weaker the hold of the central nucleus.

166

This means that the most complicated of the inert gas elements is also the least inert. The inert gas with the most complicated atom is radon. Its atoms have an electron arrangement of 2, 8, 18, 32, 18, 8. Radon, however, is made up only of radioactive isotopes, so it is a hard element to perform chemical experiments on. The next most complicated inert gas is xenon, which is stable. Its atoms have an electron arrangement of 2, 8, 18, 18, 8.

The outermost electrons in the xenon and radon atoms are far enough from the nucleus to be held not quite strongly enough. They will be given up in the presence of atoms which have a particularly strong tendency to attract electrons. The atom with the greatest tendency to attract electrons is fluorine, and in 1962 a Canadian chemist, Neil Bartlett, found it possible to form compounds of xenon and fluorine.

Since then, compounds of radon and of krypton have also been formed. Because of this, chemists don't like to use the phrase "inert gases" anymore since the atoms are not, after all, *completely* inert. The phrase "noble gases" has now become common, and there is a whole new branch of chemistry, dealing with the "noble gas compounds."

The smaller noble gas atoms are, of course, the more inert, and nothing has been found which can take electrons away from them. Argon, with the electron arrangement 2, 8, 8 in its atoms, and neon, with 2, 8, are still completely inert. And most inert of all is helium, whose atoms contain a single electron shell with two electrons (all that innermost shell will hold).

84

Why do crystals form and why always in a certain shape?

There are three states of matter under ordinary conditions: gaseous, liquid, and solid. In gases, the energy of the constituent atoms or (usually) molecules is so high, or the attraction between separate molecules is so low (or both), that the various molecules move about independently.

If the energy is decreased to a certain point, the molecules can no longer remain independent but must stay in contact. There is still enough energy, however, for the molecules to move about, slipping and sliding over each other. Such instances are liquids.

If the energy is further decreased, the separate molecules can no longer slip and slide but remain fixed in a certain orientation (though they may and do vibrate back and forth about their fixed positions). Now the substance is a solid.

In a solid, two neighboring molecules (or atoms, or ions) do not take up just any position. They fall into some regular arrangement that depends on what proportion of different particles there are, what differences in size may exist, how much external pressure there is, and so on. In sodium chloride, the sodium ions and the chloride ions are equal in number and not too different in size. In cesium fluoride, the cesium ions and fluoride ions are equal in number but the cesium ion is much the larger of the two. In magnesium chloride, the magnesium ions and chloride ions are not too different in size but there are twice as many chloride ions as magnesium ions. Each compound quite naturally packs differently because of this.

If you get a visible piece of matter made up of atoms, ions, or molecules all arranged in orderly fashion, that visible piece will have smooth surfaces meeting at fixed angles. (This is like an army formation seen from the air. You may not see the individual soldiers, but if they are well arranged you will see the platoon is in the form of a rectangle,

for instance.) The overall shape of the visible piece (or "crystal") depends on the atomic arrangement. For any given substance under a given set of conditions, the atomic arrangement is fixed and therefore the crystal is always of a given shape.

Solid substances are almost always crystalline in nature, even if they don't look it. To form a perfect crystal, you see, it is best to start with a pure substance in solution (so that strange atoms don't slip in and upset the arrangement). The solution should be cooled slowly to give atoms time to shift into array. In nature, we always have mixtures of substances so that we end up with different kinds of crystals jostling and crowding each other. What's more, if cooling is rapid so many crystals get started that no one of them has a chance to grow to more than microscopic size, and these are oriented every which way and therefore not a given shape.

It follows that we only rarely see a sizable and clear crystal in nature. Usually we have to deal with irregular pieces of material made up of microscopic crystals that we are unaware of.

There are some solid substances that are not crystalline and therefore are not really solid. Glass is an example. Liquid glass is very viscous, so that it is difficult for the ions to move about and get into orderly array. As the glass cools, the ions move more and more slowly and finally stop moving altogether, keeping whatever positions they have indefinitely.

There is no regular arrangement under such conditions, so that "solid" glass is really a "supercooled liquid." The glass may be hard and feel solid, but it has no crystalline structure and (what is a dead giveaway) it does not have a sharp melting point. So the "solid" glass just gradually softens when heated.

85

Can water be compressed?

The simplest answer to that question is that *everything* can be compressed.

As it happens, it is much easier to compress matter in gaseous form than in any other form. That is because gases are made up of molecules that are widely separated from each other. In ordinary air, for instance, the actual molecules take up something like a tenth of a percent of the total volume.

In compressing a gas, it is only necessary to push the molecules closer together against the expansive tendency of their own random motion, and squeeze out some of the empty space between the molecules. This can easily be done by human muscular effort. When you blow up a balloon, for instance, you are compressing air.

In the case of liquids and solids, the atoms and molecules composing them are just about touching. They are kept from moving still closer together by the mutual repulsion of the electrons in the outer regions of each. This represents a much stronger resistance to compression than does molecular motion in a gas.

That means that human muscles can no longer do the job, at least not noticeably.

Suppose you pour a quantity of water into a rigid container open on top and fit a nonleaking piston into the opening so that it touches the water. If you push down on the piston with all your might you will find that it will not budge noticeably. For that reason, it is often stated that water is "incompressible" and cannot be squeezed into a smaller volume.

Not so. You *do* compress the water by pushing at the piston, but not

170

enough to measure. If the pressure is made much greater than human muscles can manage, the decrease in the volume of water, or of any other liquid or solid, becomes large enough to measure. For instance, if 100 gallons of water is pressed together with a force equal to seven tons on every square inch, its volume will shrink to 96 gallons. As pressure increases further, the volume will shrink further. In such compression, the electrons are, so to speak, being pushed closer and closer to the nucleus.

If the pressure becomes great enough, say by the piled-on weight of many thousands of miles of matter under a large gravitational force, the electrostatic repulsion breaks down altogether. The electrons can no longer maintain themselves in orbit about the nucleus and are pushed away. Matter then consists of naked atomic nuclei with electrons flitting here and there in random motion.

The nuclei are much tinier than atoms and so this "degenerate matter" is again mostly open space. The pressure at the center of the earth or even of Jupiter is not large enough to form degenerate matter, but there is degenerate matter at the center of the sun.

A star made up entirely of degenerate matter can be as massive as the sun but possess no more volume than the earth. This is a "white dwarf." It can compress still further under its own gravity, till it is composed of neutrons that touch. Such a "neutron star" can have all the mass of the sun compressed into a sphere eight miles across.

And that, too, can be compressed, astronomers think, right down to the zero volume of a "black hole."

86

What is metallic hydrogen? How can hydrogen be a metal?

We all know a metal when we see it because metals have unusual properties. When smooth, they reflect light with great efficiency so that they have a "metallic luster," while nonmetals are not very reflective and have a "flat color." Metals are easy to deform, can be beaten into sheets and drawn into wires, while nonmetals are brittle and break or powder if struck. Metals conduct heat and electricity easily; nonmetals do not.

Why the difference?

In most common compounds, such as those we see all about us in the ocean and soil, the molecules are made up of atoms held firmly together by a mutual sharing of electrons. Every electron present is bound tightly to one atom or another. When this happens, a substance shows nonmetallic properties.

Hydrogen is a nonmetal by this criterion. Ordinary hydrogen consists of molecules made up of two hydrogen atoms. Each hydrogen atom has a single electron and the two that make up a molecule share the two electrons evenly. No electrons are left.

What happens when some electrons *aren't* firmly held? Consider the element potassium, for instance. Each potassium atom has nineteen electrons, arranged in four shells. Only the electrons in the outermost shell are available for sharing, and in the case of the potassium atom that means it has only one electron to share with a neighbor. This outermost electron is particularly loosely held, moreover, for between it and the central atomic nucleus which attracts it are other shells of electrons. These intermediate shells insulate the outermost electron from the central attraction.

In solid potassium, the atoms pack together closely like the pyramids of oranges you sometimes see in fruit stores. Each particular potassium atom has eight neighbors. With the outermost electron so loosely held,

172

and so many neighboring atoms so near, it is easy for any one of these outermost electrons to slip from neighbor to neighbor.

It is these loose and mobile electrons that make it possible for atoms of potassium to pack together so closely; that make it possible for it to conduct heat and electricity easily; that make it possible for it to undergo deformation. In short, these loose and mobile electrons make potassium (and other elements and mixtures that possess them) metallic.

Now remember, hydrogen, like potassium, has only one electron to share with its neighbors. There is, however, a difference. There are no insulating electrons between hydrogen's one (and only) electron and the central nucleus. The electron is therefore held a little too firmly to be mobile enough to turn hydrogen into a metal or to force its atoms to pack closely.

But what if the hydrogen gets help? What if it is forced to pack closely not by its own electronic situation but by pressure from outside? Suppose there is enough pressure to squeeze hydrogen atoms so tightly together that each atom is surrounded by eight, ten or even twelve close neighbors. The single electron of each hydrogen atom might then, despite the unusually strong attraction of the nucleus, start slipping from neighbor to neighbor. You would then have "metallic hydrogen."

In order to force hydrogen to pack so closely, it must be present in an almost pure state (the presence of other kinds of atoms would interfere) and at not too high a temperature (high temperature would cause it to expand). It must also be under enormous pressure. The one place in the solar system where the conditions are most nearly right is in the center of Jupiter, and some people think, therefore, that the interior of that planet may be made up of metallic hydrogen.

87

What is this "polywater" we are reading about?
It is still H$_2$O, so what makes it different?

A molecule of water is usually described as made up of two atoms of hydrogen and one of oxygen — H$_2$O. If this were all there were to it, it would be a small molecule with a low boiling point. Hydrogen sulfide (H$_2$S), which has a similar, but heavier molecule (because S is heavier than O), is a gas that liquefies only at $-61.8°$ C. Water, if it were just H$_2$O, would liquefy at a still lower temperature, perhaps around $-80°$ C.

But consider the shape of the water molecules. The three atoms form very nearly a right angle, with the oxygen atom at the apex. The oxygen shares two electrons with each of the two hydrogen atoms, but that share is not an even one. The oxygen has the stronger attraction for electrons, so that the electrons, with their negative electrical charge, are well over on the oxygen side of the molecule. This means that although the water molecule is electrically uncharged on the whole, the oxygen side of the molecule has a small negative charge and the two hydrogen atoms small, balancing positive charges.

Opposite charges attract. There is a tendency, then, for two neighboring water molecules to line up so that the negative oxygen end of one is adjacent to the positive hydrogen end of the next. This forms a "hydrogen bond" that is only one-twentieth as strong as the ordinary bonds that hold hydrogen and oxygen together within the molecule. This is still enough to make the water molecules "sticky."

Because of this stickiness, water molecules come together more easily and break apart with more difficulty than they would otherwise. It is necessary to heat the water to 100° C. to overcome the stickiness and bring it to a boil. If the temperature drops to 0° C., the prevalence of hydrogen bonds is such that the water molecules lock into place and freeze to ice. The temperature would have to be far colder for this to happen, were it not for the hydrogen bonds.

This does not happen to a molecule like H_2S, for instance, because the sulfur atom and hydrogen atom have a roughly equal attraction for electrons. There is no accumulation of charge on one side or another and, therefore, no "stickiness."

Next, suppose that water molecules are present in very restricted quarters — in an extremely thin glass tube, for instance. They might then jostle themselves into a tighter-than-normal approach. The oxygen atom of one molecule might be forced unusually close to the hydrogen atom of the neighboring one, so close that the hydrogen bond becomes as strong as an ordinary bond. The two molecules become one. Another molecule might latch on to this double molecule, then still another and yet another.

In the end there may be many molecules clinging tightly together, with all the hydrogens and oxygens forming regular hexagon arrangements. The resulting multiple substance is an example of a "polymer." It is "polymerized water" or, for short, "polywater." Before such a substance (first reported by Soviet chemists in 1965) can be broken up into the individual H_2O molecules of water vapor, it must be heated to about 500° C. Then, too, because the molecules are pushed so much closer together than in ordinary water, polywater has a density 1.5 times that of ordinary water.

The notion of polywater has not, however, become generally accepted. Many chemists think that what has been called polywater is really water that has picked up some impurities, or has dissolved some glass. In that case, polywater may not exist after all.

88

Why does water expand when it freezes?

We might ask first: Why is a solid solid? And why is a liquid liquid?

There is a certain attraction between the molecules of a substance that can hold them firmly together in some fixed position. It is hard to pull them apart and the substance is therefore solid.

The molecules contain energy of motion, however, and they jitter about their fixed position. As the temperature goes up, the molecules gain more and more energy, and jitter about more violently. Finally, they gain so much energy that the attraction of other molecules can no longer hold them. They break the grip and move off on their own, slipping and sliding about the other molecules. The solid has then melted; it has become a liquid.

Most solids are crystalline. That is, not only do the molecules remain fixed in place, but they are fixed in regular positions, in ranks and files. This regularity is broken up when the molecules gain enough energy to break away, and the solid melts.

Usually, the regular placing of the molecules in a crystalline solid is in a kind of close order. The molecules are crammed together with little space between them. Once the substance melts, though, the molecules, in sliding past each other, jostle and push one another. The general effect of the pushing is to force all the molecules a bit farther apart. The substance expands and its density decreases. In general, then, liquids are less dense than solids.

Putting it another way, solids expand when they melt and liquids contract when they freeze.

A lot, though, depends on just how the molecules are placed in the solid form. In ice, for instance, the water molecules are arranged in an unusually loose formation. The molecules are in a three-dimensional pattern that actually leaves "holes."

As the temperature rises, the molecules break loose and begin to move about independently, with the usual jostling and pushing. This would move them apart, except that it also moves them into the holes. By filling the holes, the liquid water takes up less room than the solid ice, despite the molecular jostling. When 1 cubic foot of ice melts, only 0.9 cubic feet of water is formed.

Because ice is less dense than water, it floats on water. A cubic foot of ice sinks in water until 0.9 cubic feet are below the water surface. This displaces 0.9 cubic feet of liquid water, which weighs as much as the entire cubic foot of ice. The ice is now buoyed up by the water and the final 0.1 cubic feet remains above the water level. This is true of ice generally. Any piece of ice will float on water with about one tenth of itself above the water surface and nine tenths of it below.

This is very fortunate for life generally. As things are, any ice that forms stays on top of a body of water. It insulates the lower depths, and cuts down the amount of heat escaping from below. As a result, the deeper water usually does not freeze even in very cold weather. Then, too, the floating ice receives the full effect of the sun in warmer weather and quickly melts.

If ice were denser than water, it would sink to the bottom as it was formed and more water would be exposed, to freeze in its turn. What's more, ice at the bottom of the body of water would get no chance to pick up the sun's warmth and melt. If ice were denser than water, our planet's water supply would be almost all frozen, even though the earth were no farther from the sun than it is now.

89

What are fuel cells? What is their advantage in generating electricity?

A fuel cell is a device for generating electricity, and, to understand its value, let's consider the words "fuel" and "cell" separately.

To generate electricity from a fuel such as coal or oil, that coal or oil must first be burned. The energy of its burning heats water to steam, which is used, in turn, to rotate a turbine through a magnetic field. That produces an electric current. In other words, we are converting the chemical energy of the fuel into heat energy and then converting the heat energy into electrical energy.

In the course of this double conversion, much of the original chemical energy is wasted. However, fuel is so cheap that even this waste doesn't prevent us from being able to produce large quantities of electricity without unusual expense.

It is also possible to convert chemical energy into electrical energy directly, without going through heat. To do so, we must make use of an electric cell. Such a cell consists of one or more solutions of chemicals into which two metal rods called electrodes are dipped. A particular chemical reaction goes on at each electrode and electrons are either released or absorbed. The electron pressure at one electrode is higher than at the other, so that if the two electrodes ar connected by a wire, electrons will flow through that wire from one electrode to the other.

Such an electron flow is an electric current, and that current will continue as long as the chemical reactions proceed in the cell. The flashlight battery is an example of such a cell.

In some cases, if an electric current is forced back through a cell after it has run down, the chemical reactions within it are made to run in reverse, so that the cell can then store chemical energy and be used to produce an electric current again. The storage battery in an automobile is an example of such a reversible cell.

Much less chemical energy is wasted in a cell, since it is there converted into electricity in a single step. However, the chemicals used in cells are all pretty expensive. Zinc goes into the making of a flashlight battery, for instance, and lead into the making of an automobile storage battery. If you tried to use enough of these metals, or similar ones, to prepare electricity for a whole city, it would cost billions of dollars a day.

A fuel cell would be a device in which the notions of fuel and the electric cell are combined. It is a cell in which the chemical reactions involve not expensive metals, but cheap fuels. The chemical energy of those fuels becomes electrical energy in a single step, with much less loss than in the usual two-step fashion. The amount of electricity available to mankind can then be greatly multiplied.

The catch is that it is difficult to prepare a fuel cell that will really work in a reliable fashion. Cells have been prepared in which electrical energy is drawn from the combination of hydrogen and oxygen, but hydrogen is still fairly expensive. Carbon monoxide has been used in place of hydrogen and it is somewhat cheaper. More recently, cells have been prepared that involve the combination of sewage and oxygen under the influence of bacterial action. Surely the thought of turning sewage into electricity is exciting and would solve two problems: cheap power and disposal of garbage.

Much remains to be done before fuel cells are really practical, but they represent one of the bright hopes of the future.

90

What are vitamins and why do we need them?

To understand vitamins we must begin with enzymes. These are molecules which act to speed certain chemical changes in the body. Enzymes come in thousands of varieties, for each chemical change is handled by a separate enzyme.

It takes only a tiny amount of enzyme to control a chemical change. Still, that tiny amount is necessary. The chemical machinery of the body is intricately interconnected, and the slowing down of a single chemical change through the shortage of some particular enzyme may result in serious illness or even death.

For the most part, enzyme molecules can easily be built up by the body from substances present in almost every article of food. There is no danger of running short of them if we are not actually starving — except for one thing.

Some enzymes contain certain unusual atom combinations as part of their structure. These atom conbinations are usually found only in enzymes and are therefore needed only in tiny quantities, since enzymes themselves are only needed in tiny quantities.

But the body must have some. If one of these atom combinations is in unusually short supply, the various enzymes that make use of it will no longer work. Certain chemical changes begin to proceed limpingly. Illness and, finally, death result.

The danger lies in the fact that although most of the enzyme molecules can be manufactured by the body, these particular atom combinations cannot. They must be absorbed, intact, from the food. A human being will sicken and die if his food does not contain tiny quantities of these unusual atom combinations.

180

When this fact was first discovered at the start of the twentieth century, the chemical nature of these atom combinations was not known. It was thought that at least some belonged to a class of substances called "amines." They were therefore called "vitamines" ("life amines") and this was later shortened to "vitamins."

Plants are the basic source of vitamins. Plants manufacture *all* their tissue substances from very simple chemicals such as carbon dioxide, water, nitrates, and so on. If they couldn't build up every single vitamin from scratch, they wouldn't be able to live.

Animals, however, can eat plants and make use of the vitamins already present in plant tissue. They don't necessarily have to make their own. Animals store the vitamins they absorb where they are most needed for enzyme work: in muscle, liver, kidney, milk, and so on. Meat-eating animals get their vitamins from the supplies painstakingly collected from plants by their plant-eating prey.

There is a certain gain in not having to make your own vitamins. Making them requires a sizable chunk of chemical machinery in every cell. If this is eliminated, there is more room, so to speak, for animals to develop machinery for the many things that plants don't have to do — nerve action, muscle contraction, kidney filtration, et cetera.

The penalty, however, is the chance of vitamin deficiency. If human beings live on a poorly chosen diet (either because it is all they like or all they can get) they may develop such diseases as beri-beri, scurvy, pellagra, or rickets — each the result of a body chemistry that is creaking to a slow halt because of enzymes that won't work for lack of a missing vitamin.

91

How did life begin?

There is no flat answer to that, since nobody was around, when life began, to serve as an eyewitness. We can make logical analyses of the problem, however.

Astronomers have come to certain decisions as to the general makeup of the universe. They find, for instance, that it is about 90 percent hydrogen and 9 percent helium. The remaining 1 percent is made up chiefly of oxygen, nitrogen, neon, argon, carbon, sulfur, silicon, and iron.

Starting with this and knowing the manner in which such elements are likely to combine, it is reasonable to conclude that the earth at the start had an atmosphere rich in certain hydrogen compounds — water vapor, ammonia, methane, hydrogen sulfide, hydrogen cyanide, and so on. There would also be an ocean of liquid water with atmospheric gases dissolved in it.

For life to form on such a world, the simple molecules that would exist in the beginning would have to combine to build up complicated molecules. In general, building up complicated molecules of many atoms out of simple molecules of a few atoms each requires an input of energy. Sunlight (particularly its ultraviolet content), shining on the ocean, would supply the necessary energy to force the small molecules to form larger ones.

But *which* larger ones?

In 1952, an American chemist, Stanley L. Miller, decided to try to find out. He prepared a mixture of substances like that which is thought to have been present in the earth's primitive atmosphere, and make certain it was completely sterile. He then exposed it for several weeks to an electric discharge that served as a source of energy. At the end of the time, he found the mixture held somewhat more complicated molecules than those with which he started. They were all molecules of types found in living tissue and included some of the amino acid building blocks of those important compounds the proteins.

Since 1952, many investigators, here and abroad, have repeated the experiment and added refinements anl elaborations. They have built up a variety of molecules by a variety of methods, and have then used those molecules as starting points for still further build-ups.

The substances so formed have all proved to be on the straight highway toward the complicated substances of life: proteins and nucleic acids. No substances have been found that differ significantly from those characteristic of living tissue.

Nothing has been formed yet that can, by the widest stretch of imagination, be called living, but scientists are working with only a few pints of liquid for a few weeks at a time. On the original earth, a whole ocean of liquid was exposed to the sun for billions of years.

Under the lash of sunlight, the molecules in the ocean grew gradually more complicated until, eventually, some molecule was somehow formed that could bring about the organization of simpler molecules into another molecule just like itself. With that, life began and continued, gradually evolving to the present state of affairs. The original forms of "life" must have been far less complex than even the simplest forms of present-day life, but they were complex enough. Scientists are working hard now to fill in the details of that "somehow" earlier in the paragraph.

It seems quite certain, however, that life developed, not as a miracle, but merely because molecules combined with each other along a line of least resistance. Life couldn't help forming under the conditions of the primitive earth any more than iron can help rusting in moist air. Any other planet that resembles the earth physically and chemically would also inevitably develop life — though not necessarily intelligent life.

92

Is silicon life possible?

All living beings from the simplest cell to the largest sequoia tree include water as by far their most common molecule. Immersed in the water are extremely complex molecules called proteins and nucleic acids which seem to be characteristic of all life as we know it. These complex molecules have a basic structure composed of chains and rings of carbon atoms. To almost all the carbons, one or more hydrogen atoms are attached. To a few of the carbons, atom combinations including such atoms as those of oxygen, nitrogen, sulfur, and phosphorus are attached.

To put it at its simplest, we can say that life as we know it is made up of hydrocarbon derivatives in water.

Can life be made up of anything else? Can we find some other kinds of molecules that will supply the complexity and versatility of life; something other than water that will supply the necessary unusual properties that serve as life's background?

Can we imagine something like water that might conceivably substitute? Liquid ammonia is closest to water in properties. On a colder planet than earth, one like Jupiter, where ammonia is very common and possibly liquid while water is solid, an ammonia-based life might be conceivable.

Then, too, hydrogen is attached in so many places on the carbon chain because it is so small that it fits anywhere, in any confined nook or cranny. Like the hydrogen atom in some ways, and almost as small, is the fluorine atom. You can have a fluorocarbon chemistry something like hydrocarbon chemistry, except that fluorocarbons are considerably stabler than their hydrocarbon analogs.

Yet perhaps on a planet hotter than earth, a flurocarbon life might be conceivable.

But what about the carbon atom? Can there be a substitute for that? Carbon can attach itself to as many as four different atoms (including other carbon atoms) in four different directions and is so small that neighboring carbon atoms are close enough, center to center, to form a strong bond. It is this which makes long chains and rings of carbon atoms stable.

Silicon most resembles carbon. It, too, can attach itself to as many as four different atoms in four different directions. However, the silicon atom is larger than the carbon atom, so that silicon-silicon combinations are less stable than carbon-carbon combinations. Long chains and rings of silicon atoms are much less likely to exist than their carbon analogs.

It is possible to have long and complicated chains of atoms in which silicon and oxygen alternate. To each silicon atom two other atoms or groups of atoms can be attached, and this sort of molecule is called a "silicone."

It may be that hydrocarbon or fluorocarbon groups can be attached to the silicone molecule, and these combinations might result in molecules large enough, delicate enough, and versatile enough to form the basis of life. In that sense, silicon life is conceivable.

But do these other forms of life actually exist somewhere in the universe? Or do forms of life exist that are based on completely alien chemistries with no points of resemblance to our own? We may never know.

93

Why did the dinosaurs die off?

For 150 million years, certain large reptiles were the most successful living creatures on earth. These are popularly called the "dinosaurs." The largest land reptiles of this sort may have weighed up to 85 tons. Large ichthyosaurs and plesiosaurs dominated the sea, while pterosaurs flew in the air with giant leathery wings up to 20 feet across.

Then, about 70 million years ago, all these great creatures became extinct. This didn't happen overnight, but it did happen in a rather short time — say a million years. Other forms of animal life, such as fish and primitive mammals and birds, weren't affected. Plant life wasn't affected either.

There have been a number of guesses as to why this happened, but they are only guesses. No one knows for certain.

Some think the climate changed. Where it had been a mild world, with swamps and shallow seas, mountains now formed. The land dried off, the sea deepened and the seasons became harsh and extreme. It is hard to believe, though, that some areas would not have remained with suitable climate. And the sea should not have been affected.

Others suggest that the early mammals feasted on dinosaur eggs and that this did the dinosaurs in. (But the sea reptiles brought forth living young.) Or perhaps grasses evolved and covered the earth, displacing earlier softer, juicier vegetation. The vegetarian dinosaurs may have lacked the kind of teeth needed to grind up the hard grasses. Then, after the vegetarian dinosaurs began to die off, the carnivorous ones, finding it harder and harder to find food, died off, too.

Then, too, perhaps the dinosaurs suddenly began experiencing an unusually large number of mutations. Since most mutations are for the worse, so many imperfect dinosaurs might have formed that the whole group of creatures died off.

This last explanation has aroused wide interest, but why should there be a sudden increase in the number of mutations?

One cause of mutations is hard radiation. Earth is constantly bombarded by cosmic rays and these might bring about the mutations that appear in organisms constantly these days. The mutation rate is not very high now, but suppose that every once in a while a particularly rich burst of radiation hits the earth.

K. D. Terry of the University of Kansas and W. H. Tucker of Rice University have pointed out that if a supernova went off fairly close to the solar system, earth might be flooded with cosmic rays. They estimated the frequency with which stars might be expected to explode into supernovas and how distant these might be, and calculated that every ten million years or so (on the average) earth might get a dose of cosmic rays about seven thousand times the present dose. Perhaps about 70 million years ago, such a packet of cosmic rays sprayed over our planet.

But if so, why should it affect only the dinosaurs? Why shouldn't it have affected other creatures as well? Perhaps it did, but it may have been that the dinosaurs were so specialized that random mutations were more likely to be lethal in their case than in other less specialized creatures.

And what kind of mutation might turn the trick? H. K. Erben of Bonn University in Germany has made one suggestion recently. He pointed out that in the last stages of the dinosaurs' existence, they were laying eggs with extremely thick shells. This may have been a disorder born of mutation. Baby dinosaurs had difficulty battering their way out of the shells and fewer and fewer were born. Between this and other similar mutations, the whole group of magnificent creatures died out.

94

What is the difference between a brain and a computer? Can a computer think?

The difference between a brain and a computer can be expressed in a single word: complexity.

The large mammalian brain is the most complicated thing, for its size, known to us. The human brain weighs three pounds, but in that three pounds are ten billion neurons and a hundred billion smaller cells. These many billions of cells are interconnected in a vastly complicated network that we can't begin to unravel as yet.

Even the most complicated computer man has yet built can't compare in intricacy with the brain. Computer switches and components number in the thousands rather than in the billions. What's more, the computer switch is just an on-off device, whereas the brain cell is itself possessed of a tremendously complex inner structure.

Can a computer think? That depends on what you mean by "think." If solving a mathematical problem is "thinking," then a computer can "think" and do so much faster than a man. Of course, most mathematical problems can be solved quite mechanically by repeating certain straightforward processes over and over again. Even the simple computers of today can be geared for that.

It is frequently said that computers solve problems only because they are "programmed" to do so. They can only do what men have them do. One must remember that human beings also can only do what they are "programmed" to do. Our genes "program" us the instant the fertilized ovum is formed, and our potentialities are limited by that "program."

Our "program" is so much more enormously complex, though, that we might like to define "thinking" in terms of the creativity that goes into writing a great play or composing a great symphony, in conceiving a brilliant scientific theory or a profound ethical judgment. In that sense, computers certainly can't think and neither can most humans.

Surely, though, if a computer can be made complex enough, it can be as creative as we. If it could be made as complex as a human brain, it could be the equivalent of a human brain and do whatever a human brain can do.

To suppose anything else is to suppose that there is more to the human brain than the matter that composes it. The brain is made up of cells in a certain arrangement and the cells are made up of atoms and molecules in certain arrangements. If anything else is there, no signs of it have ever been detected. To duplicate the material complexity of the brain is therefore to duplicate everything about it.

But how long will it take to build a computer complex enough to duplicate the human brain? Perhaps not as long as some think. Long before we approach a computer as complex as our brain, we will perhaps build a computer that is at least complex enough to design another computer more complex than itself. This more complex computer could design one still more complex and so on and so on and so on.

In other words, once we pass a certain critical point, the computers take over and there is a "complexity explosion." In a very short time thereafter, computers may exist that not only duplicate the human brain — but far surpass it.

Then what? Well, mankind is not doing a very good job of running the earth right now. Maybe, when the time comes, we ought to step gracefully aside and hand over the job to someone who can do it better. And if we don't step aside, perhaps Supercomputer will simply move in and push us aside.

95

What is the speed of thought?

That depends on what you mean by "thought."

You might mean imagination. I can imagine myself to be right here on earth and then one second later imagine myself to be on Mars or at Alpha Centauri or near some distant quasar. If that's what you mean by "thought," then you can argue that thought can have any speed up to the infinite.

Yes, but you're not *really* carried through that distance, are you? I can imagine myself present at the formation of the earth but that doesn't mean I have engaged in time travel. I can imagine myself at the center of the sun, but that doesn't mean I can really exist under those conditions.

In order for the question to have any meaning in a scientific sense, you have to define "thought" in such a way that it can have a speed that can actually be measured by physical methods.

For instance, the only reason you can think at all is because there are impulses flashing from nerve cell to nerve cell. Any action that depends upon the nervous system depends on those impulses. If you touch a hot object you snatch your hand away, but you cannot do so until the sensation of heat travels from your hand to your central nervous system and another nerve impulse then travels from your central nervous system to your muscles.

The unconscious "thought" involved — "I feel something hot, and I had better remove my hand or it will be seriously damaged" — cannot be faster than the time it takes the nerve impulse to cover the necessary round-trip distance. Therefore, we must understand the "speed of thought" to be the "speed of the nerve impulse" or there can be no answer.

190

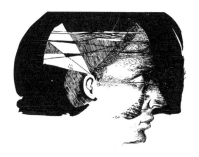

Back in 1846, a great German physiologist, Johannes Müller, in a fit of pessimism decided that the speed of the nerve impulse could never be measured. Six years later, in 1852, one of his erstwhile pupils, Hermann von Helmholtz, managed to measure it. He worked with a muscle to which the nerve was still attached. He stimulated the nerve at various points and measured the time it took for the muscle to contract. When he stimulated the nerve at a point more distant from the muscle, the contraction was delayed. From the time of delay he knew the time it had taken the nerve impulse to travel the extra distance.

The speed of the nerve impulse depends on the thickness of the nerve. The thicker the nerve, the faster it goes. It also depends on whether the nerve is insulated with a sheath of fatty material. An insulated nerve conducts the nerve impulse faster than an uninsulated one.

The mammalian nerves are the finest in the animal kingdom, and the best mammalian nerves carry the nerve impulse at a rate of about 330 feet per second or, if you prefer, 225 miles per hour.

That may seem disappointingly slow. The speed of thought is no greater than that of an old-fashioned propeller plane. But consider that a nerve impulse can go from any point in the human body to any other point and back again in less than 1/25 of a second (barring delays in processing at the central nervous system). The greatest stretch of mammalian nerve is in the 100-foot-long blue whale, and even there any possible round trip within the body can be carried out by the nerve impulse in just a little over half a second. That's fast enough.

96

What is meant by "biological clocks," and how do they work?

Sometimes you don't have to look at a clock. When you get hungry, you know it's dinner time. When you get sleepy, you know it's bedtime. If you have had a huge lunch, of course, you may go well past dinner time before getting hungry. If you have slept late or are at an exciting party, you may go well past bedtime before getting sleepy. Under ordinary conditions, though, you can come pretty close.

There is a cyclic change inside you that makes you feel hungry every so often and sleepy every so often. These changes are quite regular, so that you can measure time (rather roughly) by these cycles. Such cycles are an example of "biological clocks."

There are steady cycles in the world outside the organism. The most noticeable one is the alternation between the light of day and the darkness of night, but there is also the twice-daily rhythm of the tides which varies in amplitude with the monthly phase change of the moon, and there is the temperature cycle that varies with the day-night period and with the annual period of the seasons.

It is useful for an organism to respond to these changes. If its food is to be found by night or only in the warm season, it might as well sleep during the day or hibernate during the winter. If it is going to lay its eggs on the shore, it can do it best at the highest high tide that comes with the full moon. Even plants respond to these rhythms so that leaves curl at sunset, flowers or fruits come at particular seasons, and so on.

We can't suppose that living organisms do all this consciously. They don't say "It's nighttime, I shall sleep," or "The days are growing shorter, I shall drop my leaves." There are, rather, automatic cycles within the organism that match the astronomic cycles in the world outside. This match is produced by natural selection. Animals or plants that possess a good match do better and have a chance at more off-spring than those with a poor match, so that generation after generation the matches improve.

The inner cycles exist even on the molecular level. Body temperature shifts up and down regularly, so do the concentration of certain constituents of the blood, the susceptibility of the body to certain drugs, and so on. Most of these cycles take about a day for the completion of one up-and-down movement, and these are called "circadian rhythms," from a Latin word meaning "about a day."

Is the inner cycle controlled by the environmental rhythms? Not entirely. If an animal or plant is placed in an artificial environment in which the outside rhythm is removed — where there is constant light or constant temperature — the rhythms go on anyway. They may be less marked and may vary somewhat from a strict 24-hour cycle, but they are there. The environmental rhythms act as no more than a "fine control."

Men and women who jet across great distances find themselves in a radically different time zone, and their internal rhythms no longer match the day-night period. This gives rise to many uncomfortable symptoms until the biological clock is reset.

As to how the biological clock works. I can tell you in two words. *Nobody knows!*

It is some sort of periodic chemical reaction in the body? If so, the clock should vary with temperature or with drugs, and it doesn't. Is it something that is keyed to very subtle rhythms in the outer world that persist even when we wipe out light and temperature variations? Maybe, but if so we have not yet discovered the nature of those rhythms.

97

What is the difference between bacteria, microbes, germs, and viruses?

Bacteria are a group of one-celled organisms which are grouped by biologists under the heading "Schizomycetes." The bacterial cell has a wall, rather like those of ordinary plant cells, but lacks chlorophyll. For this reason, the bacteria are often lumped together with other chlorophyll-lacking plants and are considered to be among the "fungi."

Bacteria are distinguished from other plant cells by being extremely small. In fact, they include the smallest cells that exist. In addition, they don't have a distinct nucleus, but rather have nuclear material scattered through the cell. For this reason, they are sometimes lumped together with simple plant cells called the "blue-green algae," which also have scattered nuclear material, but which possess chlorophyll in addition.

It is becoming more and more common to group bacteria with other larger one-celled creatures, to form a class of creatures that are considered neither plants nor animals. These make up a third kingdom of life, the "protista." Some bacteria are "pathogenic," which means they cause disease. Most types, however, do not and are, indeed, often very useful. The fertility of the soil, for instance, depends to a large extent on the activity of soil-dwelling bacteria.

A "microbe" is, properly speaking, any form of microscopic life, for it comes from Greek words meaning "small life." The expression "germ" is more general still, for it means any small bit of life, even if it is part of a larger organism. For instance, that section of a seed that contains the actual living portion is the germ; thus we speak of "wheat germ."

Again, the egg and sperm, which carry the tiny sparks of life that will eventually flower into a complete organism, are called the "germ cells."

In common practice, however, both microbe and germ are used as synonyms for bacteria and, indeed, are applied particularly to disease-causing bacteria.

The word "virus" is from the Latin, meaning "poison." This dates back to the time when biologists did not know exactly what a virus was, but knew that certain preparations contained something that caused disease.

The virus differs from the bacteria and from all other organisms in not being composed of cells. It is much smaller than a cell and is only the size of a large molecule. It is made up of a coil of nucleic acid surrounded by a coat of protein. In this, it resembles the chromosomes of a cell, so that one might almost regard a virus as a "chromosome on the loose."

The chromosomes control the chemistry of the cell; and the virus, once it gets inside a cell, sets up a countercontrol of its own. Usually it can bend the chemistry of the cell to its own purposes, turning all the cell machinery to the task of forming more viruses. The cell is often killed in the process.

Viruses, unlike bacteria, lack the capacity for independent life. They can multiply only within cells. All are parasitic. The damage they do may be unnoticeable in some cases; but in other cases, serious diseases are produced.

98

How were viruses discovered?

In the 1860s, the French chemist Louis Pasteur advanced the "germ theory of disease." According to this theory, every contagious disease was caused and spread by some tiny form of life that multiplied in the sick organism, passed from that organism to a healthy one, and made it sick in turn.

In the 1860s, however, Pasteur was working with the deadly disease "rabies" (also called "hydrophobia") and discovered that, although the disease was contagious and could be contracted from the bite of a rabid animal, he could find no germ associated with it. Pasteur concluded that there was a germ all right, but that it was too small to be seen by the microscopes he had.

Other diseases also seemed to lack a germ, possibly for the same reason. An example was "tobacco mosaic disease," which attacked tobacco plants and produced a mottled mosaic pattern on the leaves as a symptom. If the leaves were mashed up, a juice could be extracted that would produce the disease in healthy tobacco plants, yet that juice contained no germ of any kind that could be seen in a microscope.

How far could microscopes be trusted at the limits of visibility? A Russian bacteriologist, Dmitri Ivanovski, tackled the matter in another way in 1892. He used a filter of unglazed porcelain that would stop anything large enough to be seen in a microscope of that day. He forced the infectious extract from diseased tobacco plants through such a filter and found that what came through could *still* infect healthy tobacco plants. Ivanovski thought that perhaps the filter was defective and didn't quite dare to conclude there were germs too small to see in the microscope.

In 1898, a Dutch botanist, Martinus Beijerinck, independently tried exactly the same experiment and got exactly the same result. He accepted the validity of the experiment and decided that whatever it was that caused tobacco mosaic disease, it consisted of particles so tiny they could pass through the filter.

Beijerinck called the disease-causing liquid a "virus" from a Latin word for "poison." Because the liquid could pass through a filter without losing its poisonous quality, he called it a "filtrable virus." The term eventually came to be applied not to the liquid but to the disease-causing particles within it. Then the adjective was dropped and the tiny disease-causing particles were simply called viruses.

But how big were the virus particles anyway? Beijerinck thought they might be not very much larger than water molecules, so that anything that would let water pass would let the virus pass, too.

This was put to the test in 1931 by a British bacteriologist, William Elford. He used collodion membranes which could be prepared with microscopic holes of any size. He passed virus-containing fluids through collodion membranes and found he could prepare a membrane with holes so tiny that the water molecules passed through, but not the virus particles. Elford found that although the original liquid transmitted the disease, what passed through that filter could no longer transmit it.

In that way, the size of the virus particle came to be known. It was smaller than the smallest cells, so small that it might only consist of a few molecules. Those molecules, however, were giant molecules.

99

Why are blood cells replaced every few months,
whereas most brain cells last for life?

The machinery of cell division is extremely complicated. The process involves numerous steps in which the nuclear membrane disappears, a small body called the centrosome divides, the chromosomes form replicas of themselves, are caught in the spindle formed by the divided centrosomes, and sort themselves out into opposite sides of the cell. A new nuclear membrane must then form at both sides while the cell constricts across the middle and divides in two.

The chemical changes involved in all this are undoubtedly even more complicated. Only in recent years have we begun to puzzle some of them out. We haven't the slightest idea yet what the direct chemical change might be, for instance, that makes cells stop dividing when the need for division is no longer present. If we knew the answer to that, we might be able to solve the problem of cancer — which is a disorder of cell growth, an inability of cells to stop dividing.

A creature as complex as man has (and must have) cells that are extremely specialized. The cells can perform certain functions that all cells can perform but can do it to an extreme. Muscle cells have developed extreme proficiency at contracting, nerve cells at conducting an electric impulse, kidney cells at allowing certain chemicals to pass through and not others. So much of the machinery in such cells must be devoted to some specialized function that there simply isn't room for the cell-division machinery. Such cells, and all cells that achieve a certain degree of specialization, have to give up dividing.

In general, once a creature has reached full growth, there is no longer need for larger size and therefore no need, in general, for more cells.

However, some cells must meet wear and tear continually. Skin cells are always undergoing contact with the outer world, cells of the intestinal membrane rub against food passing through, red blood cells against the walls of capillaries. In every case, friction and other hardships take their toll. In the case of the skin and intestinal membranes, cells in the deeper layers must retain the ability to divide so that new cells can continually replace the old cells flaking off. On the skin, in fact, surface cells die before they flake off so that the outermost layer of the skin is a dead, tough, weatherproof protection. In a place where friction is particularly great, the dead layer piles up into a callus.

Red blood cells completely lack nuclei, and, therefore, lack the cell-dividing machinery that is invariably concentrated in the nuclei. In many places in the body, however, notably in the marrow of certain bones, there are cells with nuclei which can divide and form daughter cells that can, in turn, gradually lose their nuclei and become red blood cells.

Some cells which don't ordinarily divide after adulthood is reached nevertheless retain the ability to do so, in case repairs are suddenly needed. In this way, a bone which has long stopped growing can begin to grow again after it is broken, just long enough to repair the break, and then stop. (What a pity nerve cells can't do the same thing.)

How long particular cells will live before being replaced depends, usually, on the nature and intensity of the stresses to which they are exposed, so that it is very difficult to give exact lifetimes. (The outer skin on the sole of a rat's paw has been found under certain conditions to be completely replaced in two weeks.) One exception is the red cell, which is subject to a constant unvarying battering. The human red cell has a quite predictable lifetime of about 125 days.

199

100

What is the purpose of aging?

It seems a shame to have to grow old and die, but it is apparently un-avoidable. Organisms like ourselves are actually designed to grow old and die for our cells seem to be "programmed" by their genes gradu-ally to undergo those changes with time which we call aging.

Can aging have a use? Can it be beneficial?

Well, the most striking property of life, beyond its mere existence, is its versatility. There are living things on land, in the sea, and in the air; in hot springs, in salt brines, in deserts, in jungles, in the polar wastes — everywhere. It is even possible to design environments like those we think exist on Mars or Jupiter and find simple forms of life that can manage to survive those conditions.

In order to achieve such versatility, there must be constant changes in gene combinations and in the nature of the genes themselves.

One-celled organisms divide, and each of the two daughter cells has the same genes the original cell had. If the genes were passed on as perfect copies from division to division forever, the nature of the original cell would never change no matter how often it divided and redivided. However, the copy isn't always perfect; there are random changes ("mutations") every once in a while, and gradually, from one parent cell, different strains, varieties, and eventually, species arise ("evolution"). Some of these species are more successful in a particular environment than others are, and in this way different species fill differ-ent environmental niches over the earth.

Sometimes individual one-celled organisms swap portions of chromo-somes with each other. This primitive version of sex results in changes of gene combinations, which further hastens evolutionary change. In multicellular animals, sexual reproduction, involving the cooperation of

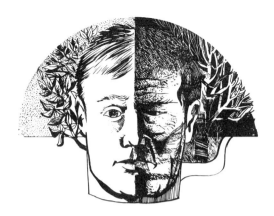

two organisms, grew more and more important. The constant production of young with their genes a random mixture of some from one parent and some from the other introduced variety beyond that possible by mutation alone. As a result, the pace of evolution was greatly hastened and species could more easily and readily spread out into new environmental niches or adapt themselves more closely to an old one so as to exploit it more efficiently than before.

The key to this, then, was the production of the young, with their new gene combinations. Some of the new combinations might be very poor, but these wouldn't last long. It would be the strikingly useful new combinations that would "make it" and crowd out the competition. In order for this to work best, however, the older generation with its "unimproved" gene combinations must not remain on the scene. To be sure, the oldsters would be bound to die off with time, thanks to accidents and the general attrition of life, but it would be more efficient to help the process along.

Those species in which the earlier generations possessed cells that were designed to age would be more efficient in getting rid of the old fogies and leaving the ground clear for youth. They would evolve faster and be more successful. We can see the disadvantage of longevity about us. The sequoia trees and the bristlecone pines that live for thousands of years are nearly extinct. The long-lived elephant isn't nearly as successful as the short-lived rat; or the long-lived tortoise as the short-lived lizard.

For the good of the species (even the human species), it seems best for the old to die that the young might live.

Sorry!

Index

(The numbers given refer to the questions, not the pages.)